The SportingNews

SELECTS

GREATEST 50 GOLFERS

Photo Credits

L = Left   C = Center   R = Right   T = Top   B = Bottom

Front cover: L, Mitch Haddad; C, Mitch Haddad; R, Robert Seale/THE SPORTING NEWS.
Back cover: Matthew Emmons.

Page 3: Bettmann/CORBIS. Page 4-5: Albert Dickson/THE SPORTING NEWS. Page 6-7: Lew Portnoy. Page 8: Malcolm Emmons. Page 9: Mitch Haddad. Page 10-11: Mitch Haddad. Page 12-13: Robert Seale/THE SPORTING NEWS. Page 14: Lew Portnoy. Page 15: Mitchell Haddad. Page 16: AP/Wide World Photos. Page 17: Malcolm Emmons. Page 18-19: AP/Wide World Photos. Page 20: Mitch Haddad. Page 21: Malcolm Emmons. Page 22-23: AP/Wide World Photos. Page 24-25: Bettmann/CORBIS. Page 26: Albert Dickson/THE SPORTING NEWS. Page 27: Mitchell Haddad. Page 28-29: Bettmann/CORBIS. Page 30: Bettmann/CORBIS. Page 31: AP/Wide World Photos. Page 32-33: AP/Wide World Photos. Page 34-35: USGA/World Golf Hall of Fame. Page 36: Lew Portnoy. Page 37: Albert Dickson/THE SPORTING NEWS. Page 38: Mitchell Haddad. Page 39: Lew Portnoy. Page 40-41: Lew Portnoy. Page 42: Mitchell Haddad. Page 43: Bettmann/CORBIS. Page 44-45: AP/Wide World Photos. Page 46-47: Bettmann/CORBIS. Page 48-49: Mitchell Haddad. Page 50-51: Bettmann/CORBIS. Page 52-53: Bettmann/CORBIS. Page 54-55: AP/Wide World Photos. Page 56-57: Bettmann/CORBIS. Page 58-59: AP/Wide World Photos. 60-61: Bettmann/CORBIS. Page 62: Mitchell Haddad. Page 63: Albert Dickson/THE SPORTING NEWS. Page 64: USGA/World Golf Hall of Fame. Page 65: AP/Wide World Photos. Page 66: Mitchell Haddad. Page 67: Lew Portnoy. Page 68-69: AP/Wide World Photos. Page 70-71: Bettmann/CORBIS. Page 72-73: Bettmann/CORBIS. Page 74-75: Lew Portnoy. Page 76: Lew Portnoy. Page 77: Albert Dickson/THE SPORTING NEWS. Page 78: Lew Portnoy. Page 79: Tomasso DeRosa for TSN. Page 80-81: Bettmann/CORBIS. Page 82: Mitchell Haddad. Page 83: Tomasso DeRosa for TSN. Page 84-85: Bettmann/CORBIS. Page 86: Mitchell Haddad. Page 87: Tomasso DeRosa for TSN. Page 88: Lew Portnoy. Page 89: Bettmann/CORBIS. Page 90-91: USGA/World Golf Hall of Fame. Page 92: Matthew Emmons. Page 93: Mitchell Haddad. Page 94: Lew Portnoy. Page 95: AP/Wide World Photos. Page 96-97: Mitchell Haddad. Page 98-99: Mitchell Haddad. Page 100: Matthew Emmons. Page 101: Mitchell Haddad. Page 102-103: Mitchell Haddad. Page 104-105: Bettmann/CORBIS. Page 106-107: Bettmann/CORBIS. Page 108: Lew Portnoy. Page 109: Albert Dickson/THE SPORTING NEWS. Page 110-111: Matthew Emmons. Page 112-113: Robert Seale/THE SPORTING NEWS. Page 115: Robert Seale/THE SPORTING NEWS. Page 116: Matthew Emmons. Page 117: Robert Seale/THE SPORTING NEWS. 118: Matthew Emmons. 119: Matthew Emmons. Page 121: Matthew Emmons. Page 122: Mitchell Haddad. Page 124: AP/Wide World Photos. Page 125: AP/Wide World Photos. Page 126: AP/Wide World Photos. Page 127: Robert Seale/THE SPORTING NEWS. Page 128: Robert Seale/THE SPORTING NEWS. Page 131: Robert Seale/THE SPORTING NEWS. Page 132: Robert Seale/THE SPORTING NEWS. Page 135: Matthew Emmons. Page 136-137: Albert Dickson/THE SPORTING NEWS. Page 139: Malcolm Emmons. Page 140: Lew Portnoy. Page 141: Lew Portnoy. Page 142: Malcolm Emmons. Page 143: Lew Portnoy. Page 144: L, Lew Portnoy. R, Lew Portnoy. Page 145: Lew Portnoy. Page 146: Matthew Emmons. Page 147: TL, Lew Portnoy. TR, Lew Portnoy. BL, Lew Portnoy. BR, Mitchell Haddad. Page 148: T, AP/Wide World Photos. B, AP/Wide World Photos. Page 149: AP/Wide World Photos. Page 150: AP/Wide World Photos. Page 151: Lew Portnoy. Page 152: TL, Mitchell Haddad. TR, Mitchell Haddad. B, Matthew Emmons. Page 153: Lew Portnoy. Page 154: Lew Portnoy. Page 155: Lew Portnoy. Page 156: L, Lew Portnoy. R, Malcolm Emmons. Page 157: Albert Dickson/THE SPORTING NEWS. Page 159: Matthew Emmons. Page 160-161: Ross Dettman for TSN. Page 163: Mitchell Haddad. Page 164: Mitchell Haddad. Page 165: Ross Dettman for TSN. Page 166: Ross Dettman for TSN. Page 168: Ross Dettman for TSN. Page 169: Mitchell Haddad. Page 170: Ross Dettman for TSN. Page 172: Mitchell Haddad. Page 173: Ross Dettman for TSN. Page 174: L, Lew Portnoy. R, Lew Portnoy.

Acknowledgements

I would like to acknowledge the following, who in one way or another, facilitated the creation of this book:

Lee Spencer, Sam Spencer, Jamie Spencer, the PGA of America, the PGA Tour, the United States Golf Association, Doc Giffin, Salvatore Johnson (whose Official U.S. Open Almanac is an invaluable resource), David Joy (author of St. Andrews and the Open Championship, whom I met both as himself and as his alter ego, Old Tom Morris, during the 2000 British Open), Tiare Bevan Peck and the World Golf Hall of Fame, the European Tour, the web site www.findagrave.com, the Golf Writers Association of America, ASAP Sports (recorders and archivists of golf press conferences), Shannon Powell and Erin Ford of Brandon Advertising in Myrtle Beach, S.C., Malcolm Campbell (author of the Scottish Golf Book), Brian Tarr and Brett Wright. Several quotes used in the book appear courtesy of The American Golfer Inc., and *The Quotable Golfer*.

I want to particularly thank Bob Parajon, creative director, and Michael Behrens, art director, at THE SPORTING NEWS. Bob spent countless hours searching for the right photos to accompany my words and give them justice. Michael's passion for the game of golf comes through on the vision and design of this book. David Walton, an assistant editor at THE SPORTING NEWS, backread and proofed the work, and oversaw responsibility in doing a book not underappreciated by me.

Dealing with hundreds of photos and making them pop off the pages is the work of THE SPORTING NEWS' Steve Romer, with an assist from Vern Kasal and Pam Speh. To them, thank you, as well.

—REID SPENCER

The SportingNews

SELECTS

GREATEST 50 GOLFERS

A Celebration of the All-Time Best

BY REID SPENCER

Defining greatness

Who's No. 1? Jack Nicklaus or Tiger Woods?

Admittedly, selecting and ranking the 50 greatest golfers of the past 150 years is an arbitrary process. But there's little or no disagreement as to the occupants of the top two rungs on the ladder—until you ask the question "Who's number one?'

It's difficult to argue against Nicklaus. As reigning U.S. Amateur champion, he finished second to Arnold Palmer in the 1960 U.S. Open at Cherry Hills Country Club in Denver.

As a PGA Tour rookie in 1962, he claimed his first tournament title at the U.S. Open at Oakmont Country Club, where he defeated Palmer in an 18-hole playoff on Palmer's home turf.

Twenty-four years later Nicklaus won his 18th major championship, The Masters, on a magical Sunday in April. In one of the longest productive careers in the history of the game, Nicklaus accumulated 70 Tour victories, 14 international wins and added 10 Senior PGA Tour triumphs after he turned 50 in 1990. Nicklaus also finished second in 19 major championships.

The flip side of that last statistic, however, is that Nicklaus failed to win 19 majors when he was in position to do so. That's a problem that has never troubled Woods, who is eight-for-eight as a closer in the majors when leading after 54 holes. Through the 2002 U.S. Open at Bethpage State Park's Black Course, Woods has won 24 of the 26 Tour events in which he held or shared the lead entering the final round.

Woods' triumph at the Black Course was his seventh in a string of 11 majors dating to the 1999 PGA Championship. Simultaneously, it was his 32nd tournament victory on Tour—at age 26, Woods is tied with Horton Smith for 12th on the all-time list. Ben Hogan, in contrast, didn't win his first title until age 27, and Nicklaus didn't reach 32 victories until age 31.

Both Woods and Nicklaus have had an enormous impact on their sport, but in different ways. Nicklaus arrived on Tour as a "villain," as an unwelcome challenger to the supremacy of Arnold Palmer, the Pied Piper of Latrobe, Pa., who marshaled an army of supporters every time he played. But it was the Nicklaus-Palmer rivalry that made casual fans tune in to golf broadcasts in the early-to-mid 1960s, only to become hooked on the intricacies of the game. And far beyond the pinnacle of his playing days, Nicklaus continues to have a profound influence worldwide as one of the foremost golf course architects of the modern era.

Woods, on the other hand, joined a Tour that had arguably the deepest reservoir or talent in golf history– and a glaring lack of personality. Not only did Woods become the dominant player on Tour in less than five full seasons (with 15 victories from 1996-1999 he tied Nick Price for most wins in the 1990s), but he also filled the personality vacuum with displays of emotion on the golf course and the seemingly limitless capacity of his will to win. In the absence of a credible rival to his dominance, Woods sends television ratings through the roof when he favors a tournament with his presence.

Both Woods and Nicklaus have provided us with spectacular moments that are burned into our collective memory—Nicklaus' one-iron shot that clanged off the flagstick and settled six inches from the cup on Pebble Beach's 17th hole to secure the 1972 U.S. Open title; Woods' birdie putt from the fringe of the 17th green at the TPC at Sawgrass en route to the first of a record three straight U.S. Amateur titles (not to mention the 60-foot "bomb" during his 2001 Players Championship victory).

Should determination and dedication to the game also be a factor in the rankings? Absolutely. That's why Hogan's return from a head-on collision with a bus to win six of his nine majors after the accident puts him solidly in third place.

Should the adulation of the golfing public count toward greatness? No question. That's why Grand Slam winner Bobby Jones, a true national hero during the Roaring Twenties, and Palmer, whose "Army" was 15,000 strong when he shot 89 in his final Masters in 2002, are fourth and fifth on the list. But nothing inspires us more than the beauty and purity of extraordinary talent, and in that respect, Woods is the greatest golfer ever to play the game. No one before him has ever exhibited both an equal degree of intelligence when working out the strategies of tournament competition AND the corresponding ability to execute his plans consistently, and without failure.

But has Woods done enough in seven seasons on Tour to offset what Nicklaus has accomplished during a lifetime of excellence?

The answer here is "Yes".

The Golfers

Tiger Woods

Born: December 30, 1975
Cypress, Calif.

No one has ever played golf better than Tiger Woods, and no other golfer has ever had a greater impact on the game. Long before his 30th birthday, Woods has already provided us with a multitude of indelible memories—three straight U.S. Amateur titles, the record-setting win at the 1997 Masters, the 15-shot rout in the 2000 U.S. Open at Pebble Beach, the "impossible" 213-yard 6-iron shot from a fairway bunker to clinch his 2000 Canadian Open victory.

Perhaps most telling about Woods is his winning percentage—he has finished first in more than 25 percent of the professional events he has entered. During his most productive years from 1962-1980, Jack Nicklaus won 67 of the 348 tournaments he played, less than 20 percent.

More than any other golfer in history, Woods has separated himself from those who pretend to be his rivals. His game is without apparent weakness—from his prodigious length off the tee to his precision iron play to his deft touch around the greens to his unerring putting stroke. Add to that mix of physical skills his extraordinary intelligence and force of will, and you have a player who towers over his competition like a colossus. Who else could have played 72 holes in the 2000 British Open at St. Andrews without hitting a bunker?

"I've won the slam before. I've won four major titles in a row, and no one has ever done that."

—Tiger Woods

33 PGA Tour wins already, including **eight majors.**

13

"Palmer and Player played superbly, but Nicklaus played a game with which I am not familiar."

—Bobby Jones

Won 18 professional major championships, and had 19 runner-up finishes in majors; in all, posted 70 PGA Tour wins.

Perhaps the strongest testament to the sustained excellence of Jack Nicklaus' career resides in one statistic—the length of time between his first professional major championship and his last. Nicklaus turned pro in 1962 with two U.S. Amateur titles and an NCAA championship in hand—not to mention a second-place finish behind Arnold Palmer in the 1960 U.S. Open at Cherry Hill Country Club in Denver, Colo.

In his first year as a PGA Tour professional, Nicklaus defeated Palmer in a playoff to claim the U.S. Open championships at vaunted Oakmont Country Club near Pittsburgh, Pa. Twenty-four years later, at Augusta National, he collected his 18th professional major title

by winning The Masters for an unprecedented sixth time. Twelve years later, as if to underline his longevity in the game, Nicklaus tied for sixth in the Masters at age 58.

The man who would become one of the greatest golfers in the history of the sport, however, arrived on the professional scene as an arch-villain, as the man who posed the most potent threat to the supremacy of Arnold Palmer. But Nicklaus gradually earned grudging respect from those who had reviled him, and eventually that respect gave way to unbridled admiration.

2 *Jack* Nicklaus

Born: **January 21, 1940**
Columbus, Ohio

Ben Hogan

Born: August 13, 1912 Dublin, Texas

Died: July 25, 1997

3

His **nine professional majors** is third all-time behind Jack Nicklaus (18) and Walter Hagen (11). Had **63 career victories** and was on four Ryder Cup teams.

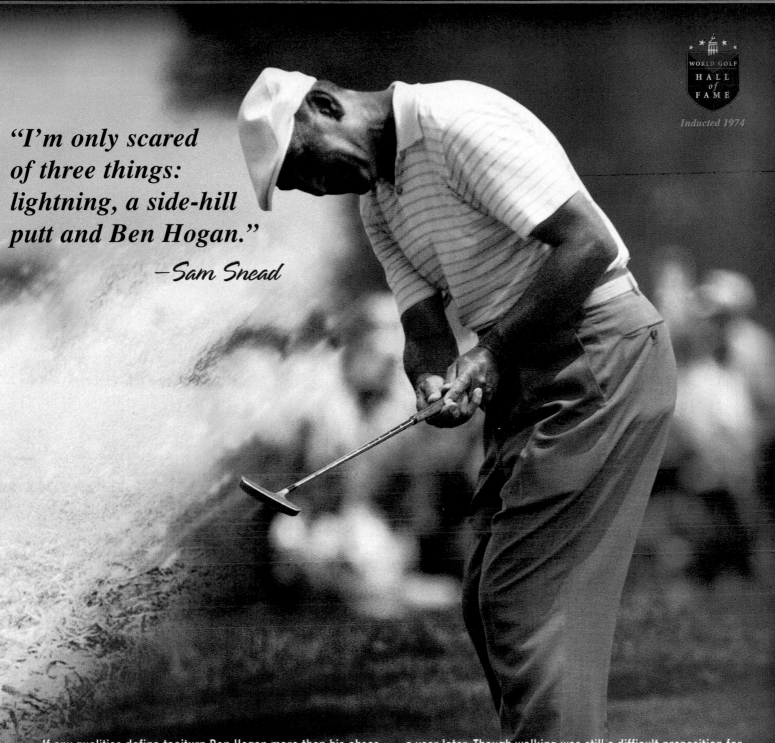

*"I'm only scared
of three things:
lightning, a side-hill
putt and Ben Hogan."*

—Sam Snead

If any qualities define taciturn Ben Hogan more than his obsession with the mechanics of the golf swing, those qualities would be his tenacity and resolve. Hogan was the greatest golfer in the world—and reigning winner of both the U.S. Open and PGA Championships—when a head-on collision with a bus near Van Horn, Texas, brought his career to a halt on February 2, 1949.

Disdaining the prognosis of doctors who doubted his ability to play professional golf again, Hogan made his comeback less than a year later. Though walking was still a difficult proposition for the man in the white cap, he came to the 72nd hole of the 1950 U.S. Open at Merion, Pa., needing par to tie Lloyd Mangrum and George Fazio for the lead at 287. Hogan rifled his now-legendary 1-iron shot to the green and two-putted for his par. The next day he shot 69 to Mangrum's 73 and Fazio's 75 to win the title in an 18-hole playoff.

4

Bobby
Jones

Born: March 17, 1902 Atlanta, Ga.

Died: December 18, 1971

"...an ultra-athlete, recognized at being better at this game than any other athlete was at his."

*—Charles Price,
Writer and Historian*

The genteel Southerner, who was born in Atlanta, Georgia, on St. Patrick's Day in 1902, was the greatest player of an era when amateur golf was still considered the pinnacle of the game. During a brief career that ended with his retirement at age 28, Robert Tyre "Bobby" Jones won a record five U.S. Amateur Championships, the first in 1924 and the last during his Grand Slam season of 1930.

The first of Jones' record-tying four U.S. Open titles came in 1923, when he defeated Bobby Cruickshank in a playoff. With three British Open titles to his credit and the 1930 British Amateur Championship also in his portfolio. Jones finished his career with 13 victories in the majors of his era.

The man who with Clifford Roberts built Augusta National Golf Club and founded the Masters Championship completed his "impregnable quadrilateral"—the Grand Slam that included the U.S. Open, U.S. Amateur, British Open and British Amateur titles—in 1930. In November of that year, Jones announced his retirement from competitive golf.

"What other people may find in poetry or art museums, I find in the flight of a good drive."

—Arnold Palmer

5

Arnold
Palmer

Born: **Sept. 10, 1929**
Latrobe, Pa.

The "King" of modern golf brought an unprecedented degree of personal magnetism to the game—as well as a legion of new golf fans who eagerly enlisted in "Arnie's Army." Arnold Palmer's ascendancy coincided with the growing importance of television as a broadcast medium for sports, and the images are indelible: Palmer hitching up his pants, taking a quick drag from a short cigarette made specially for the golf course, nearly coming out of his shoes with that ferocious, technically awkward swing of his, and firing at the flag.

The defining moment in Palmer's career came in 1960. Having already won The Masters that year, Palmer came to the final round of the U.S. Open at Cherry Hills Country Club in Denver seven shots behind third-round leader Mike Souchak. At lunch between the third and fourth rounds (during the era when the two final rounds both took place on Saturday), Palmer wondered aloud what a score of 65 would do for his chances.

Palmer proceeded to drive the green at the short par-4 first hole and finished with 65—good for a two-shot win over amateur Jack Nicklaus. That comeback embodied the famed Arnold Palmer "charge." To this day, the galleries still follow him with enthusiasm and reverence.

Two-time PGA player of the year; four times the PGA Tour's leading money-winner; has over 90 career victories, including PGA, Senior PGA and international tournaments.

7

Walter **Hagen**

Born: December 21 , 1892 Rochester, N.Y.
Died: October 5 , 1969

40 PGA victories, including 11 majors; five PGA Championships, four British Opens and two U.S. Opens.

"*All the players who have a chance to go after big money should say a silent prayer to Walter Hagen. It was Walter who made professional golf what it is.*"

— *Gene Sarazen*

Walter Hagen, the immensely talented and flamboyant pro from Rochester, N.Y., was a perfect complement to the decade during which he enjoyed his greatest success—the Roaring Twenties. All told, Hagen won 11 professional major championships, second only to Jack Nicklaus' 18, including an unprecedented string of four straight PGAs from 1924 through 1927. The first American professional to win the U.S. Open, "The Haig" did so in 1914 at Midlothian Country Club in Blue Island, Ill., where he fashioned a one-shot victory over amateur Chick Evans.

Though Hagen is famous for saying, "I never wanted to be a millionaire, just to live like one," he nevertheless earned more than $100,000 per year for tournament play and exhibitions during the 1920s. Hagen's scrambling style of play on the golf course mirrored his personal life—into trouble and safely out again.

Winner of **75 titles worldwide,** including **nine** professional **majors;** one of only five players to complete a **career Grand Slam** of golf's four professional majors.

As difficult as it must have been to find his niche in an era that included Arnold Palmer and Jack Nicklaus, Gary Player did exactly that. Player established an identity as the "Black Knight" for his choice of all-black golf outfits that "soaked up the sun."

The son of a South African gold miner, Player won his first major, the British Open at Muirfield, in 1959 at age 23. With subsequent victories at Carnoustie in 1968 and Royal Lytham & St. Anne's in 1974, Player is the only 20th-century golfer to take possession of the Claret Jug in three different decades.

Player won his first Masters title in 1961, thanks to a double bogey from favorite Arnold Palmer on the final hole. Seventeen years later, at age 42, Player won his third Masters by a single stroke over Hubert Green, Rod Funseth and Tom Watson. His only U.S. Open victory came in 1965 at Bellerive Country Club in St. Louis, where he defeated Aussie Kel Nagle in a playoff. Player donated his $25,000 first-place check to charity.

8

WORLD GOLF
HALL
of
FAME

Inducted 1974

*"Golf is a puzzle
without an answer.
I've played golf
for forty years
and I still haven't
the slightest idea
how to play."*

—Gary Player

Gary

Player

Alan

Born: November 1, 1935
Johannesburg, South Africa

Six British Open victories, and runner-up on four other British Opens; one U.S. Open Championship.

WORLD GOLF
HALL
of
FAME

Inducted 1974

Recognized as the foremost member of golf's first Great Triumvirate (which included James Braid and J.H. Taylor), Harry Vardon won the first of his record six British Open Championships in 1896 at Muirfield, where he defeated Taylor in a 36-hole playoff.

The first Englishman to win the Open, Vardon repeated the feat in 1897 and 1898. In 1900 he claimed his only U.S. Open title at Chicago Golf Club in Wheaton, Ill. Playing against doctors' advice in the 1903

British Open, Vardon won the championships by six shots over his brother, Tom Vardon, using a gutta percha ball instead of the traditional "feathery."

But Vardon was on the verge of fainting several times during the final round and a short time later was diagnosed with tuberculosis. His failing health diminished what otherwise might have been an even more distinguished career.

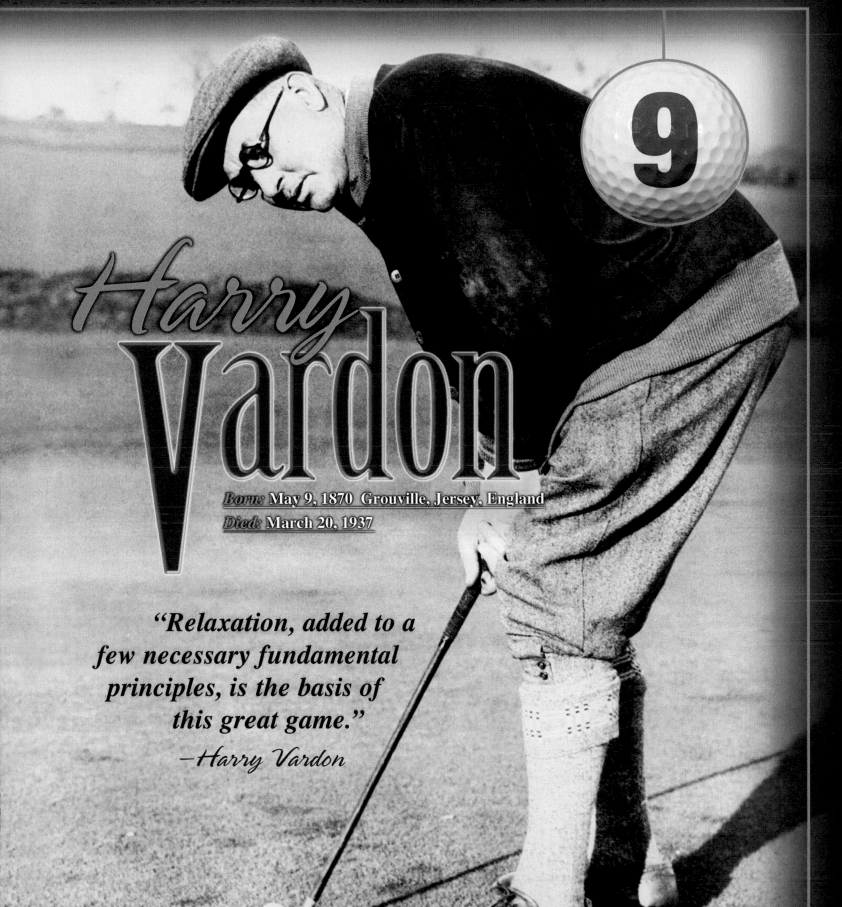

Harry Vardon

Born: May 9, 1870 Grouville, Jersey, England
Died: March 20, 1937

"Relaxation, added to a few necessary fundamental principles, is the basis of this great game."

—Harry Vardon

"Byron Nelson accomplished things on the pro Tour that never have been and never will be approached again."

—Arnold Palmer

NELSON

Byron Nelson

10

Born: February 12, 1912
Fort Worth, Texas

54 PGA Tour wins and five major championships – two Masters, two PGAs and one U.S. Open.

10 UNDER PAR

In 1945, Byron Nelson enjoyed what many will argue was the greatest year in the history of professional golf. Admittedly, many of his foremost rivals were involved in the war effort (from which Nelson was excluded because his blood was slow to coagulate), but Nelson's accomplishments that season are no less extraordinary.

First and foremost, he established two records that seem every bit as "untouchable" as Joe DiMaggio's 56-game hitting streak. Nelson triumphed in 18 tournaments in 1945, and remarkably, he won 11 of those events in a row, starting with the Miami Four-Ball (with partner Jug McSpaden) and ending with the Canadian Open. In between, Nelson beat Sam Snead in a playoff to win the Charlotte Open and claimed the PGA Championship with a 4-and-3 victory over Sam Byrd at Moraine Country Club in Dayton, Ohio.

It was also in 1945 that Nelson posted 19 straight scores under 70 and established the record for lowest scoring average in PGA Tour history with a 68.33. A mark that stood until Tiger Woods eclipsed it with a 67.79 scoring average in 2000.

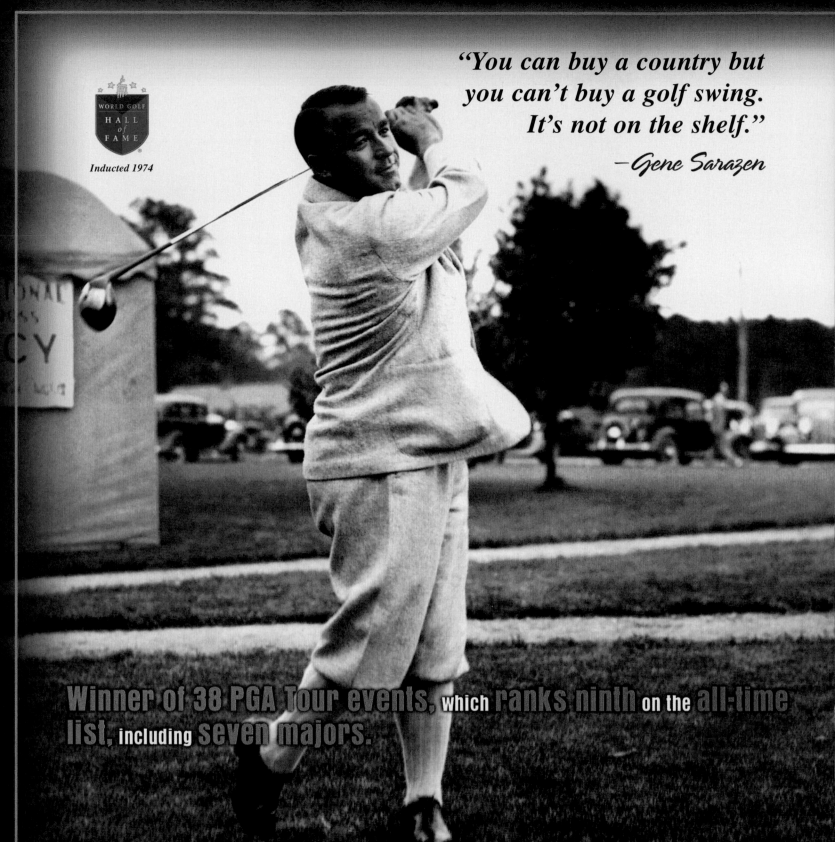

"You can buy a country but you can't buy a golf swing. It's not on the shelf."

—Gene Sarazen

Winner of 38 PGA Tour events, which **ranks ninth** on the **all-time list,** including **seven majors.**

"The Squire" (born Eugenio Saraceni) was the first player to win the Grand Slam of all four professional majors, though the fledgling Masters wasn't considered a major when Sarazen won it in 1935.

In fact, Sarazen helped define The Masters as a tournament of enormous import with his version of the "shot heard round the world." Sarazen arrived at the par-5 15th hole at Augusta National in the final round of the 1935 championship trailing long-hitting Craig Wood by three strokes. After a drive of approximately 260 yards,

Sarazen faced a 220-yard carry over water to the green.

"Hurry up, will ya? I've got a date tonight," shouted playing partner Walter Hagen from across the fairway, as Sarazen and his caddy debated club selection. Moments later Sarazen chose a 4-wood and launched his second shot toward the flagstick. With tournament founder Bobby Jones watching from a vantage point beside the 15th green, Sarazen holed the "double eagle" to tie Wood for the lead. The following day, Sarazen won the title in a 36-hole playoff.

11

Gene Sarazen

Born: February 27, 1902 New York, NY
Died: May 13, 1999

Born into a golfing family, Willie Anderson was the son of Thomas Anderson, the head greenskeeper and starter for the West Links at North Berwick. An apprentice clubmaker at age 14, Willie emigrated to America with his father and brother Tom Jr. in 1896. A year later he entered his first U.S. Open at age 17 and finished second to Joe Lloyd over 36 holes at Chicago Golf Club.

Anderson won the first of his record four U.S. Open titles in 1901 at Myopia Hunt Club in Boston. The 1903 Open at Baltusrol (N.J.), where he signed on as the club's first golf professional in 1898, began a streak of three straight championships for Anderson, the only player ever to win three U.S. Opens in a row. He was also the first golfer to break 300 over 72 holes in an American event—when he shot 299 to win the 1902 Western Open.

Anderson's focused, intense demeanor on the golf course provided a stark contrast to his convivial lifestyle after the round was over. Affable and well-liked by fellow pros, Anderson died in 1910 at age 31.

"Most likely, had he lived longer, Willie would have set a record for Open Championships that would never be beaten."

—*Alex Smith, who finished second to Anderson in two U.S. Opens.*

Willie Anderson

12

Born: **October 21, 1879 North Berwick, Scotland**

Died: **October 25, 1910**

Four U.S. Open titles and four victories in the Western Open, the second most prestigious professional event of his era.

34 PGA Tour Wins including eight major championships.

"I'm not going to get it close —I'm going to make it."

—Tom Watson,
to caddie Bruce Edwards before
chipping in to win the 1982 U.S. Open.

WORLD GOLF
HALL
of
FAME

Inducted 1988

36

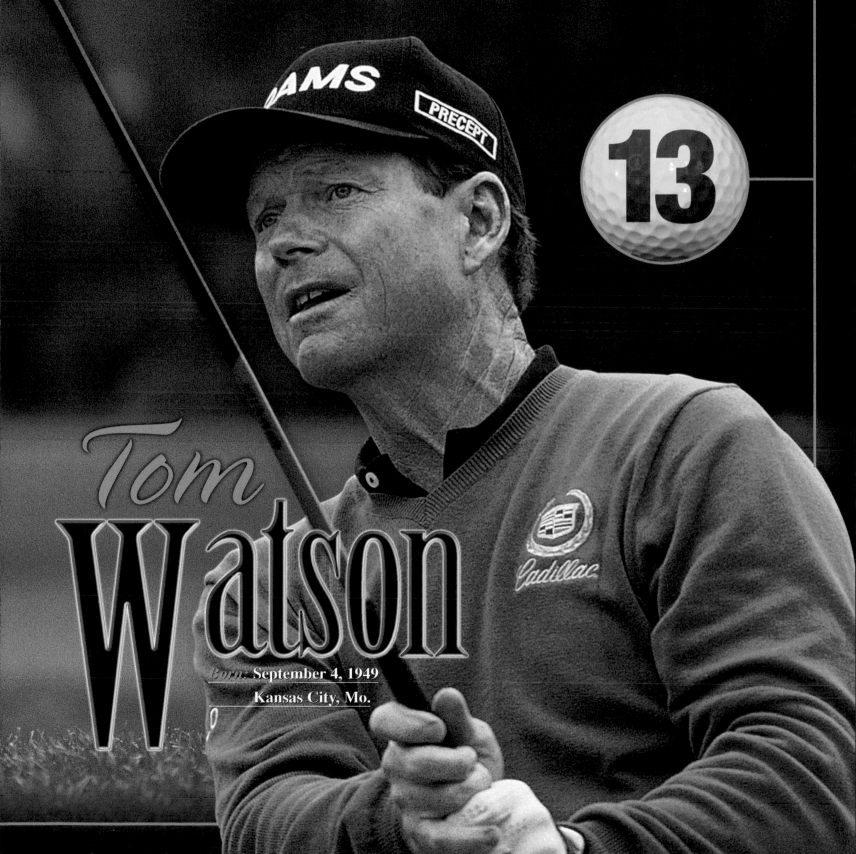

Tom Watson can point to two defining moments in a career that has spanned three decades. In the 1977 British Open at Turnberry's Ailsa Course, Watson outlasted Jack Nicklaus in what became known as the "Duel in the Sun." Watson and Nicklaus shot identical rounds of 68-70-65 to enter the final round tied at seven under par. With four holes left, Watson trailed by one shot, but he holed a 60-foot birdie putt at the 15th to catch Nicklaus. The Stanford alumnus won the championship with a birdie at the 17th, which propelled him to a final-round 65 and a one-shot win over the Golden Bear.

Five years later, Watson would deprive Nicklaus of a 19th major championship when he chipped in from the rough behind the green at Pebble Beach's par-3 17th hole—once again the 71st hole of a major championship. The unlikely shot, which turned a probable bogey into a birdie, gave Watson his only U.S. Open title by two strokes.

Tom
Watson

Born: September 4, 1949
Kansas City, Mo.

13

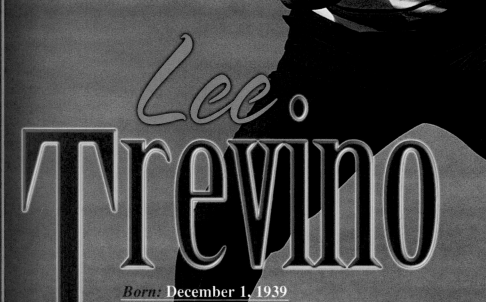

Winner of **six majors** — two U.S. Opens, two PGAs and two British Opens; 27 PGA Tour victories.

14

Lee
Trevino

Born: December 1, 1939
Dallas, Texas

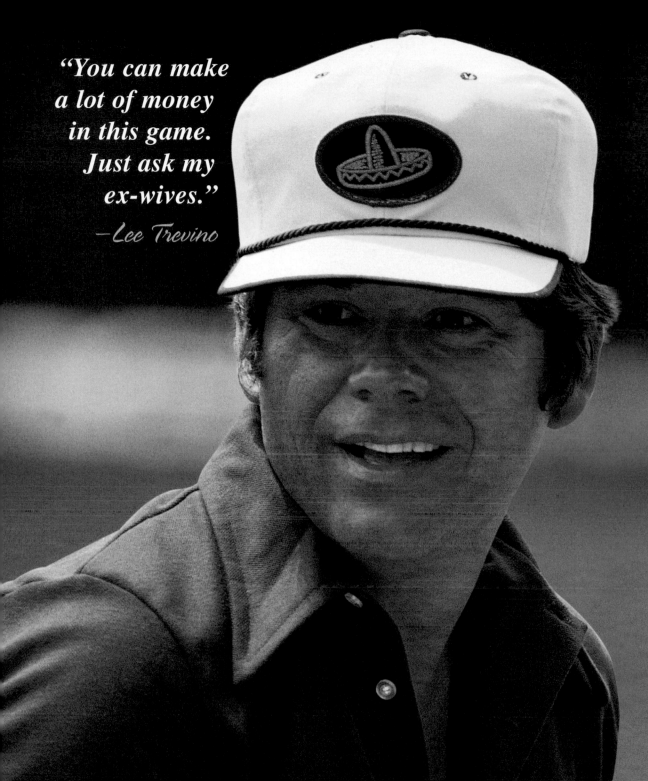

"You can make a lot of money in this game. Just ask my ex-wives."

—Lee Trevino

Dubbed the Merry Mex for his steady stream of one-liners, Lee Buck Trevino fashioned a golf career that has taken him from the caddyshack to the World Golf Hall of Fame. A seventh-grade dropout, Trevino helped support his family by caddying and by gambling on the golf course. After a four-year stint in the Marine Corps, Trevino turned pro in 1960 and joined the PGA Tour in 1967.

His first victory came in America's most important championship, the U.S. Open. At the 1968 championship, Trevino became the first player in Open history to post four scores in the 60s.

Shooting 69-68-69-69--275 at the par-70 course, Trevino finished four shots ahead of runner-up Jack Nicklaus.

Trevino collected his second U.S. Open title in 1971 and followed that with victories in the British Open and Canadian Open. Until Tiger Woods duplicated the feat in 2000, Trevino was the only player to have accomplished that trifecta. A year later, Trevino chipped in to save par at the 71st hole of the British Open at Muirfield, thereby preventing Nicklaus, who finished one stroke behind, from winning the third leg of the Grand Slam. Trevino added PGA Championships to his portfolio in 1974 and 1984.

"*Golf puts a man's character on the anvil and his richest qualities—patience, poise, restraint— to the flame.*"

—*Billy Casper*

51 Tour wins, sixth on the all-time list, including **two U.S. Opens** and one Masters Championship.

Billy Casper 15

Born: **June 24, 1931**
San Diego, Calif.

Casper hasn't received the recognition he deserves for his accomplishments on the golf course, perhaps because he made the headlines more often for his quirky diets—a regimen that included whalemeat steaks, for example—than for his excellent play.

Golf fans were reluctant to embrace Casper, who often appeared aloof. To distance himself from the galleries even farther, Casper upset the "King," Arnold Palmer, in the 1966 U.S. Open at the Olympic Club in San Francisco. With nine holes remaining in the championship, Casper trailed Palmer, his playing partner, by seven shots. But Palmer began focusing on breaking Ben Hogan's U.S. Open scoring record of 276 and forgot about Casper.

By the 14th hole, Casper had trimmed the lead to five, and with birdies to Palmer's bogeys on 15 and 16, he trailed by one as they came to the 17th. With a par to another Palmer bogey at the long par-four, Casper pulled even. He won the title the next day in an 18-hole playoff with a 69 to Palmer's 73—in a round that saw a six-shot swing in Casper's favor on the back nine.

6 PGA Tour titles, including **five Majors;** also
has **64 European Tour titles** to his credit.

WORLD GOLF
HALL
of
FAME

Inducted 1997

16

Seve
Ballesteros

Born: **April 9, 1957**
Pedrena, Spain

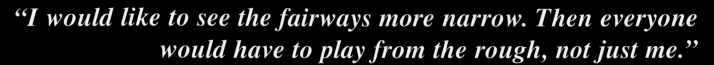

> ## *"I would like to see the fairways more narrow. Then everyone would have to play from the rough, not just me."*
>
> *—Seve Ballesteros*

He brought the fist pump to the sedate world of golf long before Tiger Woods arrived on the scene. More than any other player, he made golf fans throughout the world care about the Ryder Cup. He was a magician around the greens—because he missed them so often. And he inspired an entire generation of Spanish golfers to compete with the game's elite.

Severiano Ballesteros was a virtual unknown when he tied Jack Nicklaus for second place in the 1976 British Open at Royal Birkdale—six shots behind runaway winner Johnny Miller. A mere three years later, with all three of his golf professional brothers in the gallery, Ballesteros would claim the first of his three Open titles at Royal Lytham & St. Anne's.

In 1984, Ballesteros birdied the 72nd hole at St. Andrews to beat Tom Watson and Bernhard Langer by two shots. Seve returned to Royal Lytham in 1988 and won the Open by two strokes over Nick Price.

17

Francis
Ouimet

Born: May 8, 1893 Brookline, Mass.

Died: September 2, 1967

WORLD GOLF
HALL
of
FAME

Inducted 1974

"It is customary to receive a security for this trophy, but in this case, the only security which the USGA will demand is that Francis Ouimet keeps up his game."

—*John Reid,*
presenting the U.S. Open
trophy in 1913.

The unlikeliest of U.S. Open champions and the first American-born player to win the title, 20-year-old amateur Francis Ouimet forever changed the face of golf in the United States with his stunning 1913 victory over two British Goliaths, Harry Vardon and Ted Ray.

A former caddie who grew up across the street from The Country Club in Brookline, Mass., site of the 1913 championship, Ouimet arrived at the 71st hole needing a par and a birdie to catch the two British pros, who already had posted 304 for the four rounds. Ouimet banged in a curling 15-foot birdie putt on the 17th and saved par at the final hole to join the playoff. In front of a gallery of more than 5,000 spectators, Ouimet won the title the next day with a 72 to Vardon's 77 and Ray's 78.

The following year Ouimet won the U.S. Amateur Championship, a feat he repeated in 1931. Two years later he was stripped of his amateur standing for opening a sporting goods store, but that decision was subsequently reversed. Ouimet was an eight-time member of the United States Walker Cup team from the inception of the event in 1922 through 1934.

John H. Taylor

Born: March 19, 1871 North Devon, England
Died: February 10, 1963

18

J.H. Taylor (left), non-playing captain of the 1933
British Ryder Cup Team, receives from the Prince of
Wales, the Ryder Cup, after the British team's victory
over the American golfers at Southport, England.

"You'll see more of Taylor, and then you'll know why he beat me, and why he will beat all the best of the day."

—*Andrew Kirkaldy, legendary Scotsman*

Renowned for his unerring accuracy, John H. Taylor was a dominant force in the British Open for 21 years. A member of the Great Triumvirate (above) that included fellow Englishman Harry Vardon (left) and Scotsman James Braid (right), Taylor captured the first of his five Open titles in 1894 at Sandwich. A year later, he won his second at St. Andrews, by four shots over Alexander Herd.

When the Open returned to St. Andrews in 1900, Taylor was again champion. He equaled the course record of 77 in the second round and went on to defeat Vardon by eight shots. Taylor won the Open twice more, in 1909 and 1913, before World War I would necessitate a five-year suspension of the championship, starting in 1915.

The turn of the century marked golf's growth as an international sport, and Taylor was in the vanguard of players who excelled outside the United Kingdom. He won the French Open twice, the German Open once and finished second to Vardon in the 1900 U.S. Open.

19

Nick

Faldo

Born: **July 18, 1957**

Welwyn Garden City, England

Pilloried in the British press for his tendency to choke under pressure early in his career, the man who was cruelly dubbed "Foldo" did anything but that in the 1987 British Open at Muirfield. With 18 straight pars in the final round, Faldo edged American Paul Azinger, who bogeyed the final two holes to lose the championship by a single shot.

Accompanied during his peak years by female caddie Fanny Sunesson, Faldo won his second Open at St. Andrews in 1990 with a total of 18-under-par 270, an Old Course record that stood until 2000, when Tiger Woods posted 269 over four rounds. In 1992, Faldo claimed his second title at Muirfield and third overall with a one-shot win over American John Cook.

Faldo's three Masters championships were each to a great degree dependent on the kindness of others. In 1989 he beat Scott Hoch on the second hole of sudden death, after Hoch missed a two-foot put for the win on the first playoff hole. A year later, Faldo defeated Raymond Floyd in a playoff, when Floyd pulled his approach to Augusta's 11th (the second playoff hole) into the pond. And in 1996, Faldo took advantage of Greg Norman's collapse to overcome a six-shot deficit entering the final round.

"One of the great compliments I heard is that Tiger watched tapes of me playing at St. Andrews and went on to win there."

— Nick Faldo

Owner of **six major titles,** including **three Masters.**

40 PGA Tour victories, including one Masters and two U.S. Opens.

"I'd give the world to have a swing like that."

—Bobby Jones

20

Cary Middlecoff

Born: **January 26, 1921 Halls, Tenn.**

Died: **September 1, 1998**

Trained as a dentist, Dr. Cary Middlecoff was seduced by the lure of professional golf—at least, that's the way his family looked at it. An All-American golfer at the University of Mississippi in 1939, Middlecoff graduated from the Tennessee College of Dentistry in 1944 and embarked on an 18-month hitch in the military, where, according to Army records, he filled more than 12,000 teeth.

After his discharge in 1946, Middlecoff worked briefly in his father's dental practice, but his success in amateur golf convinced him to try his hand as a professional. His success was almost immediate. By 1947, the former Tennessee Amateur champion had won three professional events, and in 1949 be bagged his first major, the U.S. Open at Medinah (Ill.) Country Club, where he endured an hour-long wait to see whether his 286 total would stand up.

Middlecoff won the Masters in 1955 and claimed his second U.S. Open title in 1956 at Oak Hill Country Club in Rochester, N.Y., the championship perhaps best remembered for Ben Hogan's miss of a 30-inch par putt on the 71st hole. Middlecoff edged Hogan and Julius Boros by a stroke.

21

Peter

Thomson

Born: **August 23, 1929**
Melbourne, Australia

WORLD GOLF
HALL *of* FAME

Inducted 1988

"The most important facets of golf are careful planning, calm and clear thinking and the ordinary logic of common sense."

— Peter Thomson

The only golfer other than Young Tom Morris to win three consecutive British Opens, Thomson raised the Claret Jug five times in the 12 years from 1954-1965. His first title came at Royal Birkdale in 1954, where he bested Sidney Scott, Dai Rees and Bobby Locke by one shot.

The even-tempered Aussie successfully defended his championship the following year at St. Andrews and again in 1956 at Hoylake. After finishing second to Locke at St. Andrews in 1957, Thomson returned to championship form in 1958 at Royal Lytham & St. Anne's, where he defeated Dave Thomas by four strokes in a 36-hole playoff.

Thomson's most impressive Open victory, however, may have come in 1965 at Southport, England, where he outlasted runners-up Brian Huggett and Christy O'Connor and a field full of American stars. In addition to his five majors, Thompson had 26 European Tour victories, 19 Australian, and 11 Senior PGA Tour wins.

"Action before thought is the ruination of most shots."
— Tommy Armour

WORLD GOLF
HALL of FAME
Inducted 1976

22

Tommy
Armour

Born: September 24, 1895 Edinburgh, Scotland
Died: September 11, 1968

One of golf's most respected teachers and clubmakers, the Silver Scot compiled an international record that included three major championships. But Armour would have had no career in golf at all had he not regained sight in his right eye—he had been blinded by a mustard gas explosion while serving in the Tank Corps during World War I. Only after a six-month convalescence did his right eye recover.

Three years after moving to the United States and turning pro in 1924, Armour became the last Scotsman to win the U.S. Open, when he defeated "Lighthorse" Harry Cooper in an 18-hole playoff at Oakmont Country Club. Armour finished 3-4-4-3-4-3 (one under par over Oakmont's daunting final six holes) to tie Cooper at 301 at the end of regulation play.

Though he often partook of the New York nightlife with such legendary carousers as Babe Ruth and Walter Hagen, Armour added a PGA Championship to his portfolio in 1930 with a 1-up victory in the final over his friend, Gene Sarazen, at Fresh Meadow Country Club in Flushing, N.Y. A player who favored difficult courses, Armour won the first British Open held at Carnoustie in 1931.

In a relatively brief career from 1924-1935, Armour won 24 events, including three Canadian Opens and One Western Open title.

The only Scotsman in golf's first Great Triumvirate, James Braid won five British Opens during the decade 1901-1910, with four coming in the six-year span from 1905-1910. After finishing third at the 1900 Open at St. Andrews, Braid acquired the aluminum-headed putter that would transform his game.

In 1901, he beat Harry Vardon by three shots at Muirfield, and in 1905 he pulled away to a five-shot win over J.H. Taylor and Rowland Jones at St. Andrews. When the Open returned to Muirfield and St. Andrews—in 1906 and 1910, respectively—Braid was champion again. In between, in 1908, he thrashed the field to the tune of an eight-stroke victory over Tom Ball at Prestwick.

After his retirement from competitive golf in 1912, Braid embarked on a new career—as an innovative and prolific golf course architect. Among his designs is one of the most beautiful, and difficult, layouts in the world—Carnoustie.

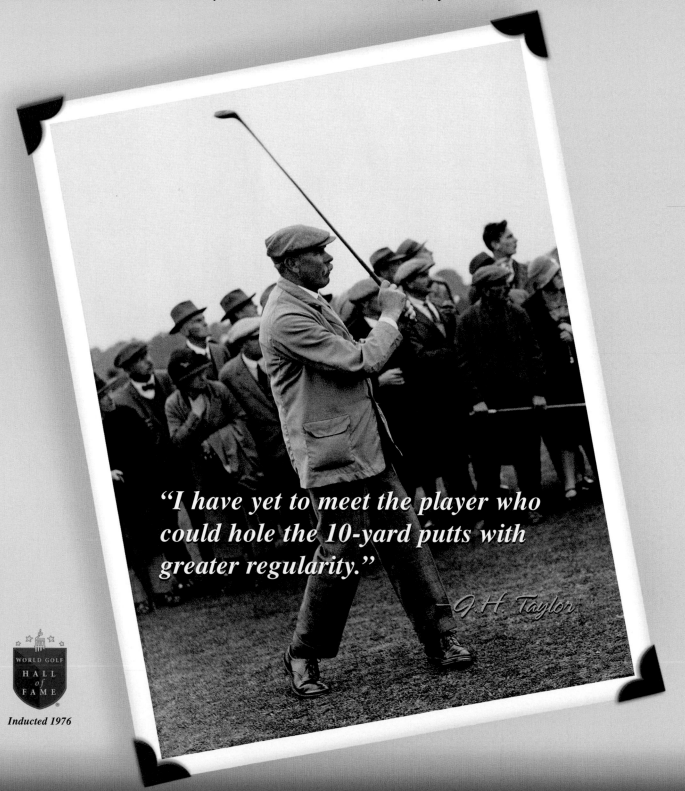

"I have yet to meet the player who could hole the 10-yard putts with greater regularity."

—*J.H. Taylor*

23

James
Braid

Born: February 6, 1870 Earlsferry, Fife, Scotland
Died: November 27, 1950

Five British Open titles, won the **British Professional Match Play Championship four times** and the **French Open** once.

"It's not your life. It's not your wife. It's just a game."

—Lloyd Mangrum

For Lloyd Mangrum, the golf course was a much friendlier place than the battlefield. As a staff sergeant in the Third Army in World War II, Mangrum suffered a broken arm and two shrapnel wounds, but the veteran of the Battle of the Bulge returned to the action on the links in 1946, having won four Battle Stars and three Purple Hearts.

It was in 1946 that Mangrum had another sort of epic battle, when he defeated Byron Nelson and Vic Ghezzi in a 36-hole playoff for the U.S. Open Championship at Canterbury Golf Club in Cleveland, Ohio. Paired with Nelson in the final round of the first Open since 1941, and with Ghezzi already in the clubhouse at 284, Mangrum parred the last three holes to make the playoff, as Nelson bogeyed the final two.

All three players shot 72 over the first 18 holes of the playoff. In the afternoon round, Mangrum was three shots behind Nelson and Ghezzi through 12 holes but rallied with birdies on 13, 15 and 16 to post his second 72 and win the title. Nelson and Ghezzi each finished the second playoff round at 73. In 1950 Mangrum was part of another historic three-way playoff for the U.S. Open Championships but in that case, he and George Fazio fell victim to a resurgent Ben Hogan.

24

Lloyd Mangrum

Born: August 1, 1914 Trenton, Texas
Died: November 17, 1973

36 PGA Tour titles, good for 10th on the all-time list.

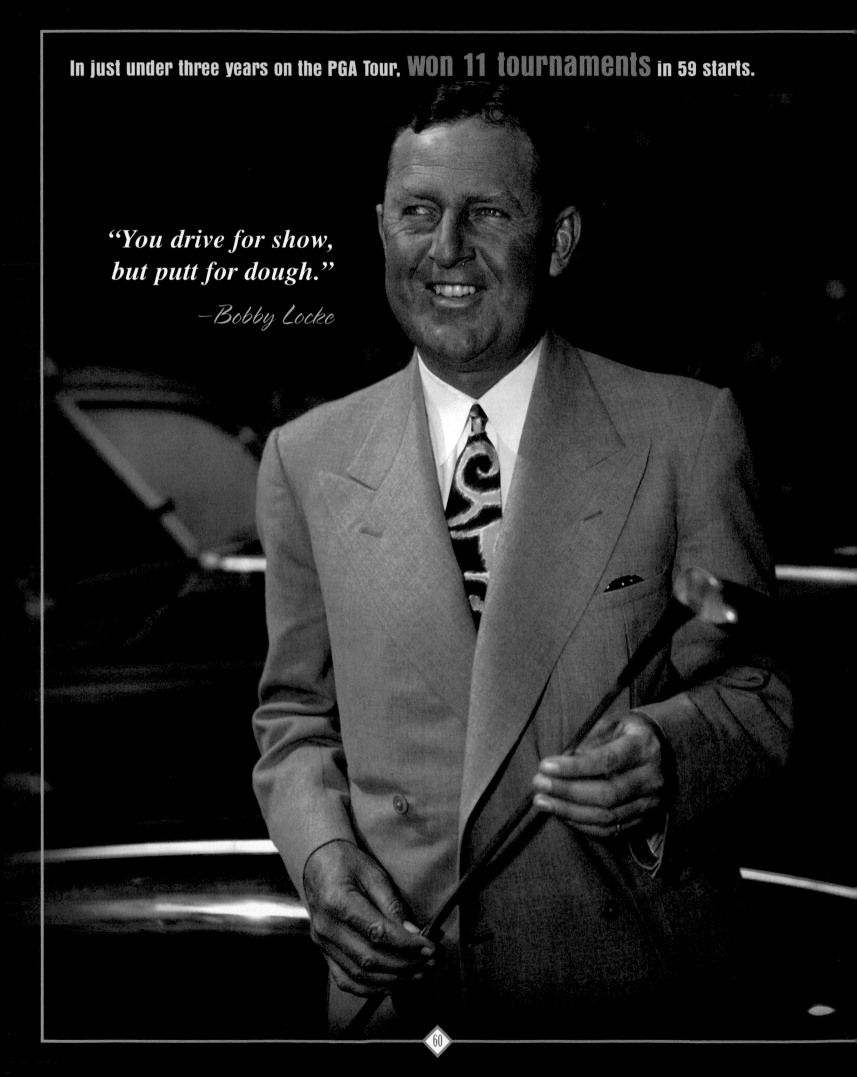

In just under three years on the PGA Tour, **won 11 tournaments** in 59 starts.

"You drive for show,
but putt for dough."

—Bobby Locke

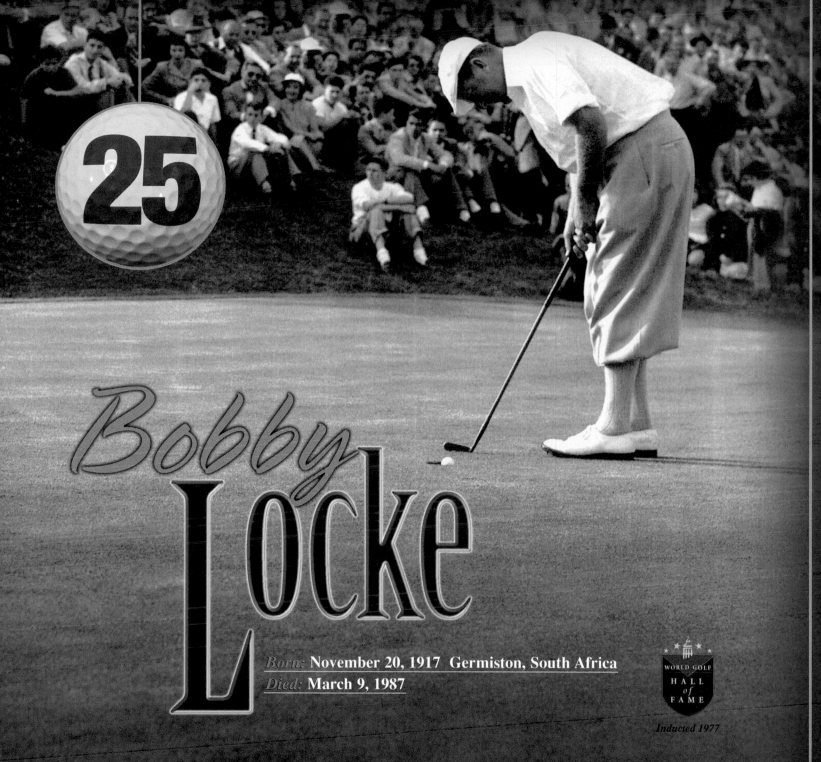

25

Bobby Locke

Born: November 20, 1917 Germiston, South Africa
Died: March 9, 1987

Known as one of the greatest putters ever to play the game, Arthur D'Arcy "Bobby" Locke won four British Open Championships in an eight-year span from 1949-1957 and paved the way for the great South African players who followed him—Gary Player, Ernie Els and Retief Goosen being the foremost among them.

Locke's history with the British Open, however, dates back to 1936. Despite a successful amateur career, Locke chose to enter the mining industry rather than to pursue a career in professional golf. But a business trip to London in 1936 coincided

with the British Open at Hoylake. Locke entered, won the amateur medal at age 18 and turned pro two years later.

World War II interrupted Locke's golf career. After logging more than 2,000 hours in the air as part of a bomber crew, Locke returned to golf in 1946, playing a series of exhibition matches against Sam Snead. Locke beat the Slammer 12 times and lost twice. He won back-to-back British Opens in 1949 and 1950, claimed the title again in 1952 and in 1957 ended Peter Thomson's Open streak at three straight with a three-shot win at St. Andrews.

"The game was easy for me as a kid. I had to play a while to find out how hard it is."

—Raymond Floyd

26

Raymond
Floyd

Born: **September 4, 1942**
Fort Bragg, N.C.

Fellow competitors know what will happen when Raymond Floyd's name rises to the top of a leaderboard. With an icy stare that grows in intensity as he closes in on victory, Floyd deserves his reputation as one of the great frontrunners in the game.

Floyd first made his mark as a PGA Tour rookie in 1963 when he won the St. Petersburg Open in his 11th start. But in the early stages of his career, Floyd was more apt to party than to practice, and his game suffered. Between 1963 and 1969, Floyd claimed but one title, the 1965 St. Paul Open, but 1969 brought renewed resolve and dedication to the game. Floyd won three times that year and captured his first major, the PGA Championship at NCR Country Club in Dayton, Ohio.

Floyd added a Masters title in 1976 with a record-tying 271 total that stood until Tiger Woods posted 270 in 1997. He claimed another PGA Championship in 1982 and won the U.S. Open at Shinnecock Hills in 1986 at age 43. Floyd's best finish in the British Open—the only leg of the career Grand Slam he lacks—came in 1978 when he tied for second with Ben Crenshaw, Tom Kite and Simon Owen, two shots behind Jack Nicklaus.

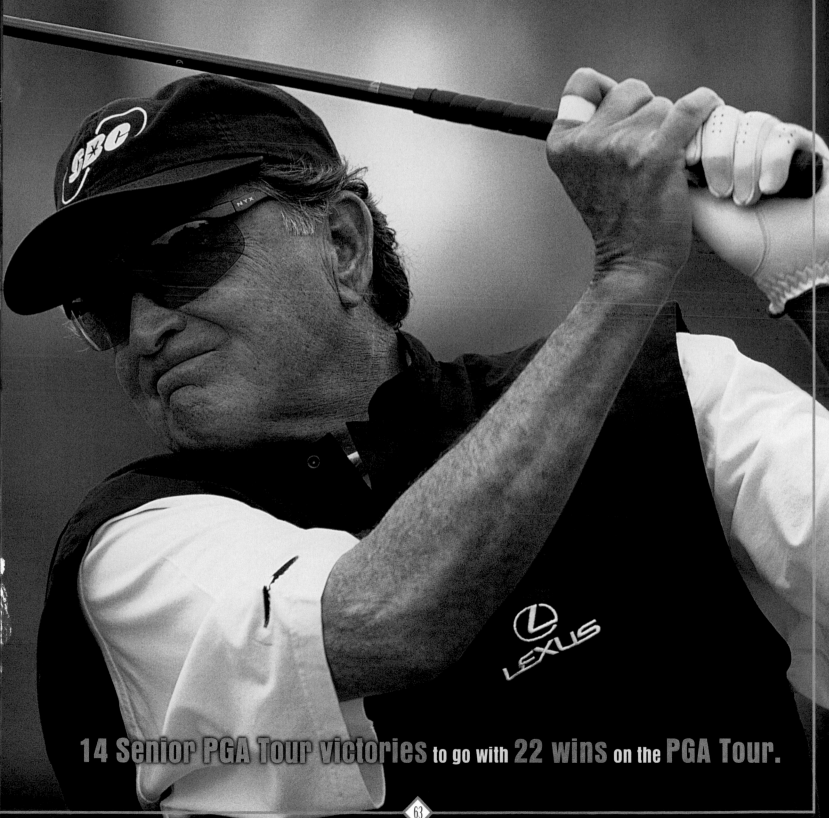

14 Senior PGA Tour victories to go with 22 wins on the PGA Tour.

Horton Smith

Born: May 22, 1908 Springfield, Mo.
Died: October 15, 1963

Won 30 PGA Tour events during his relatively short career; led the money list in 1929 with just over $7,600.

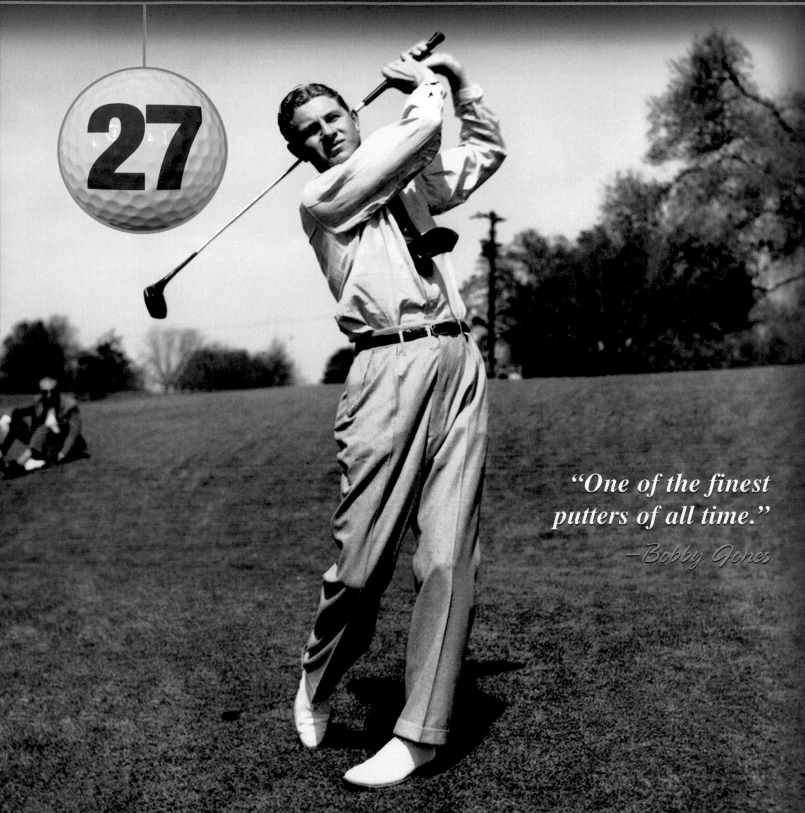

27

"One of the finest putters of all time."

—*Bobby Jones*

Though Horton Smith attained his greatest renown as the winner of the first Masters tournament in 1934, he enjoyed his most prolific year as a golf professional in 1929, when he won eight of 22 events at age 21 and finished second six times. But it is for The Masters that Smith will be remembered, though the tournament did not acquire its official name until five years after he won the event for the first time.

Playing in what was originally called the Augusta National Invitational, Smith sank a 20-foot birdie putt on the 71st hole and parred the last to beat Craig Wood, hard-luck loser of the first two Masters, by a single shot. In the 1934 tournament, the contestants played what is now the back nine first. In the fall of that year, the nines were reversed to their present configuration.

With his deft touch on the greens working to perfection, Smith became the first two-time winner of The Masters in 1936 when he birdied 14 and 15 in a driving rainstorm-the former with a 50-foot chip shot-to edge Lighthorse Harry Cooper by one stroke.

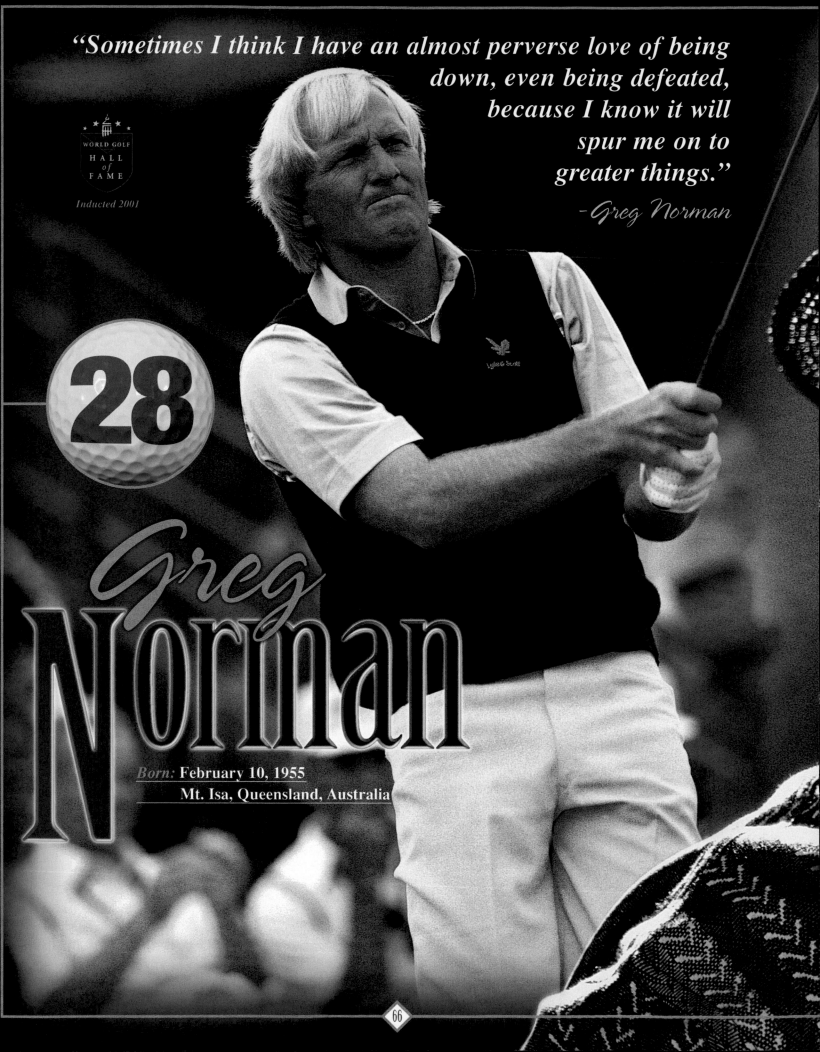

"*Sometimes I think I have an almost perverse love of being down, even being defeated, because I know it will spur me on to greater things.*"

- Greg Norman

WORLD GOLF
HALL of FAME

Inducted 2001

28

Greg
Norman

Born: **February 10, 1955**
Mt. Isa, Queensland, Australia

Two British Open titles, 57 **international titles and** 18 **Tour titles.**

It is Greg Norman's unfortunate fate to be remembered not for the two major championships he won, but for the multitude that eluded him. Norman was runner-up in majors no less than seven times, and lost each of the four professional majors in a playoff at least once.

No defeat was more galling to the Great White Shark than the 1996 Masters—the tournament he covets most—where Norman shot a major-championship record-tying 63 in the first round and led Nick Faldo by six shots entering the final day of play. Norman staggered home with a 78 as Faldo won by five.

Who can forget Larry Mize's lightning bolt in the Georgia Pines, the implausible chip-in from the right of the 11th green that wrested a playoff victory from Norman in the 1987 Masters? Who can forget Bob Tway, sinking a bunker shot on the final hole at Inverness to rob the Shark of a chance to win the 1986 PGA Championship? Add to the list the 1984 and 1995 U.S. Opens, the 1986 Masters and the 1993 PGA—all within Norman's grasp, none converted. But for the rub of the green, the star-crossed Norman could have been one of the legends of the game with as many as nine major titles.

Bob Hope referred to him as the best amateur comedian in the world. Herbert Warren Wind dubbed him "The Wardrobe" for his flamboyant, sometimes outrageous choices in golf attire. And yet, Ben Hogan considered Jimmy Demaret the most underrated professional golfer of his era, a man who could work magic with a golf ball.

It wasn't until 1938 that Demaret finally made his career choice—between professional golfer and nightclub singer. Two years later he won his first Masters championship by four shots over Lloyd Mangrum. Demaret enjoyed his most productive year in 1947, when he posted six victories, won the Vardon Trophy and led the money list.

In 1950, Demaret shot 69 in the final round of The Masters to grab a two-shot win over Jim Ferrier, who skied to a 75 on the last day. At the presentation ceremony that afternoon, Demaret, in typical fashion, grabbed the microphone and began singing. Demaret was a threat to win well into his 40s; he claimed three titles in 1957, his last year on Tour, at age 47.

"Golf and sex are the only things you can enjoy without being good at them."

—Jimmy Demaret

29

Jimmy Demaret

Born: **May 10, 1910 Houston, Texas**

Died: **December 8, 1983**

"You'll never win golf tournaments until you learn how to score well when you're playing badly."

—Jim Barnes

WORLD GOLF
HALL
of
FAME

Inducted 1989

In the **nine-year stretch** from 1920 through 1928, he **finished in the top eight seven times** at the British Open.

The only player ever to receive the U.S. Open trophy from the President of the United States, "Long Jim" Barnes (so named for his 6-foot-4 frame and his prodigious drives) won four major titles in an era that featured stars of much higher magnitude—Jones, Hagen and Sarazen, for instance.

A wire-to-wire winner of the 1921 U.S. Open at Columbia Country Club in Chevy Chase, Md., Barnes cruised to a nine-shot victory over Walter Hagen and Fred McLeod after an opening round 69. His winning margin in the

Open was the largest of the 20th century (until Tiger Woods destroyed the field by 15 strokes at Pebble Beach in 2000). President Warren G. Harding attended the final round and was first to shake Barnes hand as he left the 18th green.

Barnes won the PGA Championship in 1916 with a 1-up victory over Jock Hutchison in the final. The next time the event was played, in 1919, Barnes claimed the trophy again with a 6-and-5 triumph over McLeod. He won his only British Open in 1925, by one stroke over Archie Compston and Ted Ray.

Jim Barnes

30

Born: **April 8, 1886 Lelant, Cornwall, England**

Died: **May 24, 1966**

As a golf professional in the early 20th century, iconoclastic Henry Cotton was anything but ordinary—he didn't need the money he was playing for. Born to a wealthy family, Cotton nevertheless pursued a career in golf and did as much to elevate the profession in the British Isles as Walter Hagen did for his American compatriots in the United States.

Cotton won the first of his three British Open championships in 1934, and in doing so set a single-round scoring record for the event with a 65 in the second round at Royal St. George's. Three years later, against a field that included the entire American Ryder Cup team, he fired a final-round 71 in howling winds and cold rain at Carnoustie generally considered "one of the finest rounds ever played in the Open" to edge R.A. Whitcombe for the title by two strokes.

World War II intervened and put a hold on what otherwise might have been an even more formidable career, but "The Maestro" returned to win the 1948 Open at Muirfield, where he fashioned an impressive five-stroke victory over defending champion Fred Daly. A renowned teacher and golf course designer, Cotton was knighted on New Year's Day 1988, nine days after his death.

WORLD GOLF
HALL
of
FAME

Inducted 1980

30 victories on the European Tour; **three British Match Play Championships.**

"*Golfers have analyzed the game in order to find 'the secret.' There is no secret.*"

—Sir Henry Cotton

Henry Cotton

Born: January 26, 1907 Holmes Chapel, Cheshire, England
Died: December 22, 1987

24 PGA Tour wins; USGA Junior Amateur champion 1964.

Johnny Miller

Born: April 29, 1947
San Francisco, Calif.

32

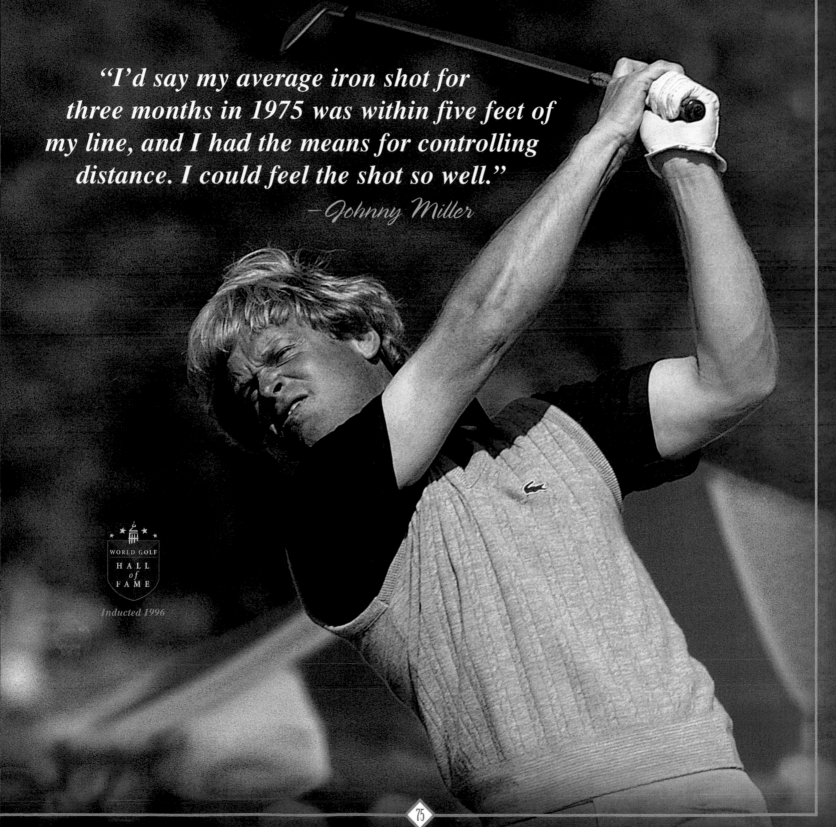

What's the greatest round of golf ever played in major championship competition? Given the timing and the circumstances, Johnny Miller's performance in the final round of the 1973 U.S. Open at Oakmont set a standard that remains unequaled. No other player has ever shot 63 on the last day of a major to win the title.

After a disappointing 76 in the third round, Miller trailed Arnold Palmer, Julius Boros, Jerry Heard and John Schlee by six shots. But Miller birdied the first four holes at the "Monster" and closed with birdies at 11, 12, 13 and 15 to edge Schlee by a stroke. Miller hit all 18 greens that day and used 29 putts (despite one three-putt). On 10 of the 18 holes, he rifled his approach shot within 15 feet of the flagstick.

Miller also authored a come-from-behind victory in the 1976 British Open, but the two years between his two majors were the most remarkable of an otherwise nondescript career. In 1974 Miller won eight tournaments and topped the money list—he was the only player other than Jack Nicklaus or Tom Watson to do so from 1971-1980. In 1975 he won four times and finished second to Nicklaus in earnings.

"I'd say my average iron shot for three months in 1975 was within five feet of my line, and I had the means for controlling distance. I could feel the shot so well."

—Johnny Miller

WORLD GOLF
HALL
of
FAME

Inducted 1996

"When I got onto the Tour, I relished the harder courses because I just felt I was going to try harder."

—Hale Irwin

A master of the long iron shot and a perennial contender on golf's most difficult courses, Irwin is the only player ever to win the U.S. Open exactly three times. (Willie Anderson, Bobby Jones, Ben Hogan and Jack Nicklaus claimed four titles each). In what became known as the "Massacre at Winged Foot," Irwin notched his first Open championship in 1974. His seven-over-par total of 287 was two better than Forrest Fezler's 289.

He followed that championship five years later with a U.S. Open victory at Inverness, where Irwin weathered a final-round 75 to defeat Jerry Pate and Gary Player by two shots. In 1990, he received a special exemption from the USGA to compete in the Open at Medinah (Ill.) Country Club and made the most of it. Six strokes down to Mike Donald with nine holes to play, Irwin staged a rally that ended with a 50-foot birdie putt on the 72nd hole.

Donald faltered on the inward nine and ended regulation play tied with Irwin at eight-under-par 280. Both men shot 74 in an 18-hole playoff the next day, and for the first time in its history, the U.S. Open went to sudden death. Irwin made short work of Donald with a birdie on the first extra hole to become, at 45, the oldest player ever to win the Open.

33

WORLD GOLF
HALL
of
FAME

Inducted 1992

Hale

Irwin

Born: **June 3, 1945**
Joplin, Mo.

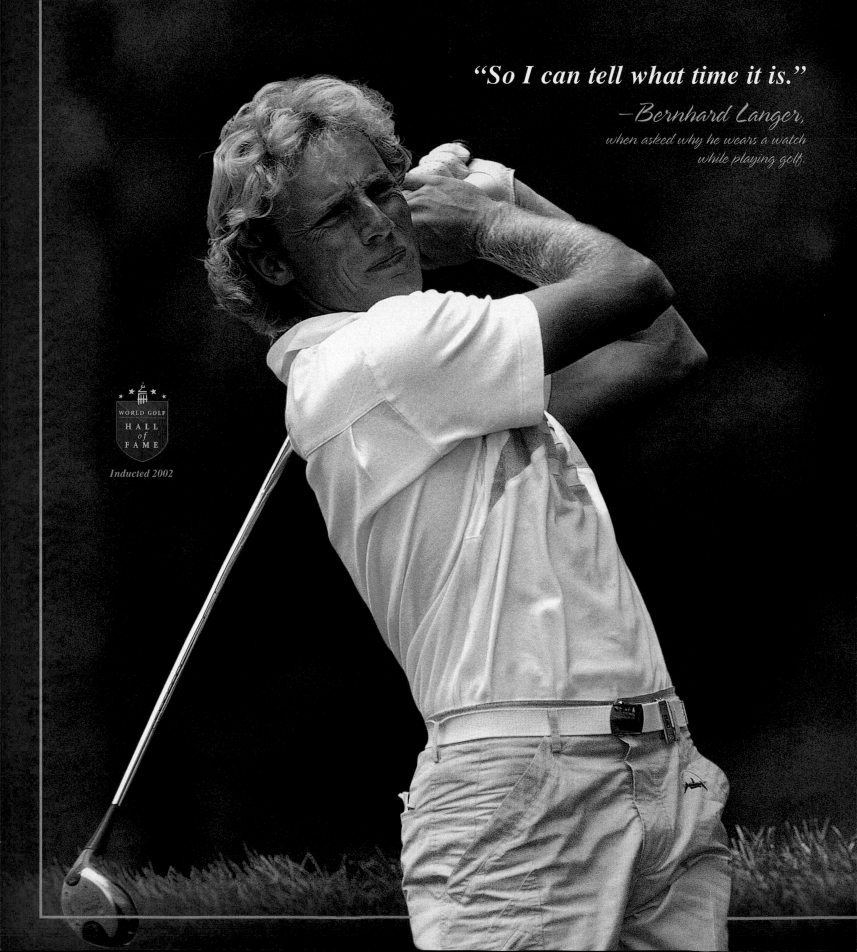

Two Masters titles and 42 wins on the European Tour; 10-time European Ryder Cup team member.

"So I can tell what time it is."

—Bernhard Langer,
when asked why he wears a watch
while playing golf.

WORLD GOLF
HALL
of
FAME

Inducted 2002

Bernhard Langer

Born: August 27, 1957
Anhausen, Germany

34

Of the 198 PGA Tour events he entered from 1981 through 2001, Bernhard Langer won exactly three—but two of them were majors. Langer, who turned pro in 1972, held off three of the game's superstars (Raymond Floyd, Curtis Strange and Seve Ballesteros) to win the 1985 Masters by two shots. A week later he defeated Bobby Wadkins in a playoff at the Sea Pines Heritage Classic; Langer is the last player to follow a Masters win with a victory in the next tournament on the schedule.

Langer missed the cut in his first Masters in 1982 and did not play in 1983, but in the 19 years since, he has played on the weekend at Augusta in April. In the 1993 Masters remembered for Chip Beck's inglorious decision not to go for the 15th green in two in the final round, Langer finished four shots ahead of runner-up Beck, who was roasted in the press for his conservative play.

Throughout the years, Langer has employed a variety of unconventional putting techniques to battle the "yips" that pose a constant threat to his career. Nevertheless, he has remained remarkably consistent as he enters his fourth decade as a professional.

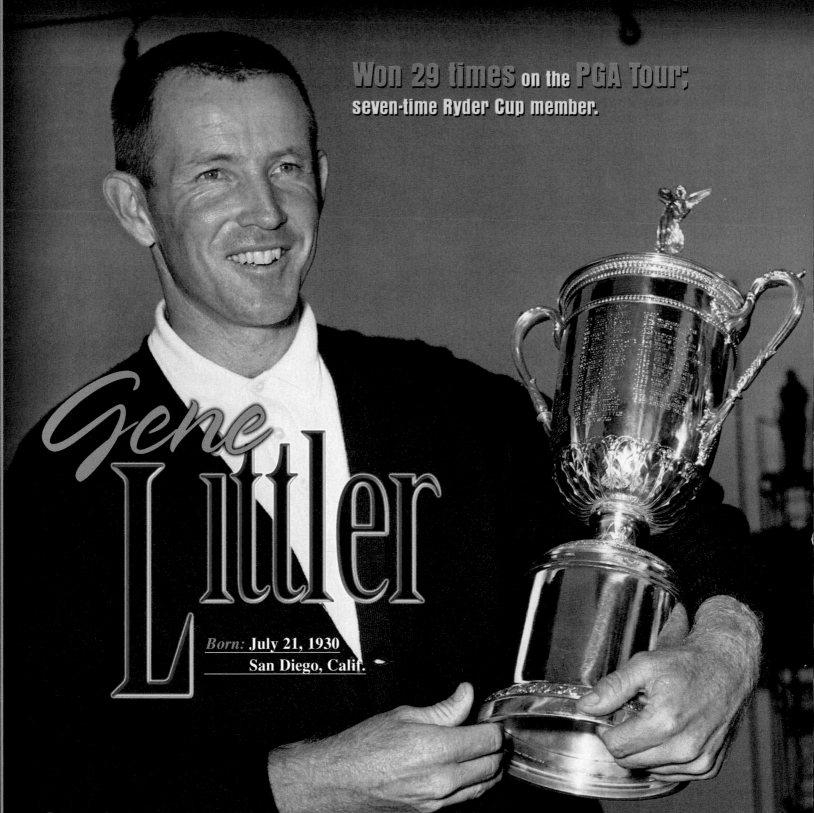

Gene Littler

Born: **July 21, 1930**
San Diego, Calif.

Economy of motion, economy of emotion and economy of language characterized Gene Littler's successful career as a professional golfer. Nicknamed "Gene the Machine," he had a seemingly effortless nature to his smooth swing, Littler won 29 times on the PGA Tour.

The 1953 U.S. Amateur champ added a U.S. Open crown to his resume in 1961, when he edged Doug Sanders and Bob Goalby by a stroke. With birdies at Oakland Hills Country Club's 11th and 13th holes, Littler posted a final-round 68, then waited in the clubhouse to see if his 281 total would stand up against a Doug Sanders' rally.

Sanders needed two birdies over the last three holes to catch Littler and got one at the 16th, but his birdie attempts at 17 and 18—the latter a chip shot—both were close misses.

The 1961 Open was Littler's only major title, but he developed a special fondness for the elite Tournament of Champions, which he won during his first three full years on Tour, staring in 1955.

Littler battled cancer of the lymph system in 1972 and returned from surgery to win the St. Louis Open in 1973. That accomplishment earned him both the Bob Jones and Ben Hogan Awards in 1973.

35

WORLD GOLF
HALL
of
FAME

Inducted 1990

"*Golf is not a game of great shots. It's a game of the most misses. The people who win make the smallest mistakes.*"

—*Gene Littler*

"Mickelson's a terrific player. As soon as Mickelson breaks through and wins one or two majors, he'll be a force to reckon with every time."

—Jack Nicklaus

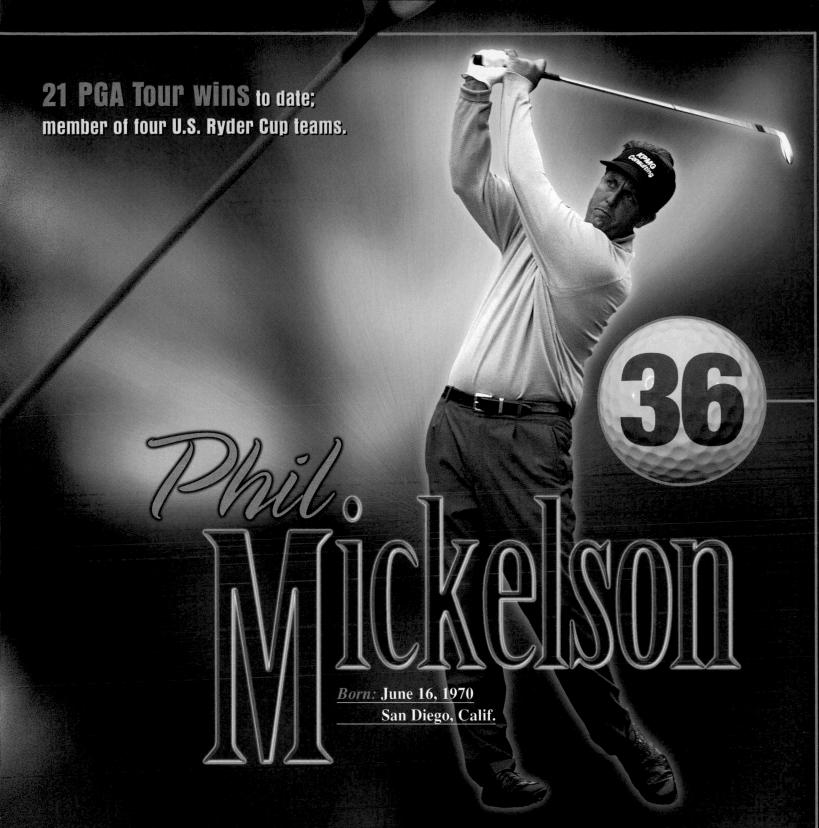

21 PGA Tour wins to date; member of four U.S. Ryder Cup teams.

Phil Mickelson

36

Born: **June 16, 1970**
San Diego, Calif.

Will Phil Mickelson fulfill his potential as one of the great talents of the game, or will he remain the 21st century's answer to Tom Weiskopf? In all probability, he'll answer that question when—and if—he wins a major championship.

Perhaps Mickelson's career would have been different had the final three holes of the 1999 U.S. Open not gone the way they did. Mickelson arrived at the long par-four 16th with a one-shot lead over Payne Stewart and appeared to have the upper hand when the players reached the green. Stewart faced a 25-foot downhill par putt, while Mickelson had a much more benign eight-footer to save his par. But Stewart shocked Mickelson by holing his putt, and Mickelson pulled his attempt to the right to lose the lead.

Mickelson missed a short birdie putt at 17, where Stewart sank an even shorter putt to gain a one-shot advantage. On the 18th green, Mickelson watched in disbelief as Stewart stroked a 15-foot par putt into the center of the cup to claim the championship. Through the 2002 U.S. Open, Mickelson had finished second or third in eight majors, a record for a non-winner.

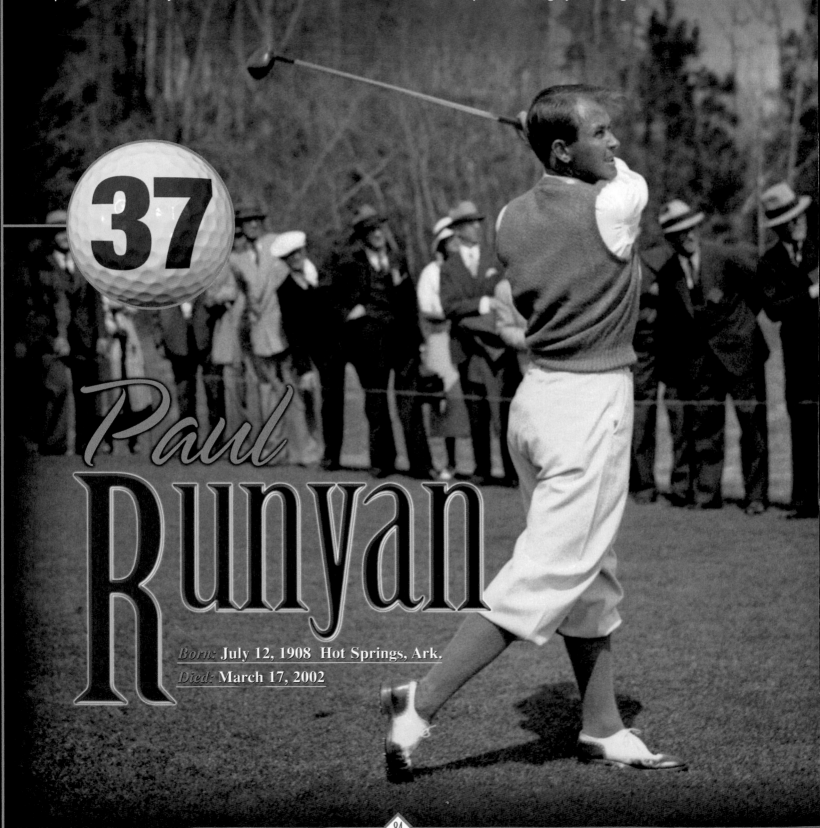

A short hitter who shared the nickname "Little Poison" with a contemporary in professional baseball, Paul Runyan overcame the limitations of his 5-foot-7, 125-pound frame with unerring accuracy and a remarkable short game.

He won the first of his two PGA Championships in 1934, when he defeated Craig Wood over 38 holes at Park Country Club in Williamsville, N.Y. Runyan claimed his second PGA title in 1938 with a lopsided 8-and-7 victory over favored Sam Snead in the final.

Runyan, whose killer instinct was better suited to match play, was 24 under par for the 196 holes he played during that championship, and in one stretch, he negotiated 64 consecutive holes at par or better.

The son of a dairy farmer, Runyan enjoyed his best season during the depths of the depression, in 1933, when he won nine events. He was the Tour's money leader in 1934—the first year official statistics were kept in that category—with a grand total of $6,767.

37

Paul
Runyan

Born: July 12, 1908 Hot Springs, Ark.
Died: March 17, 2002

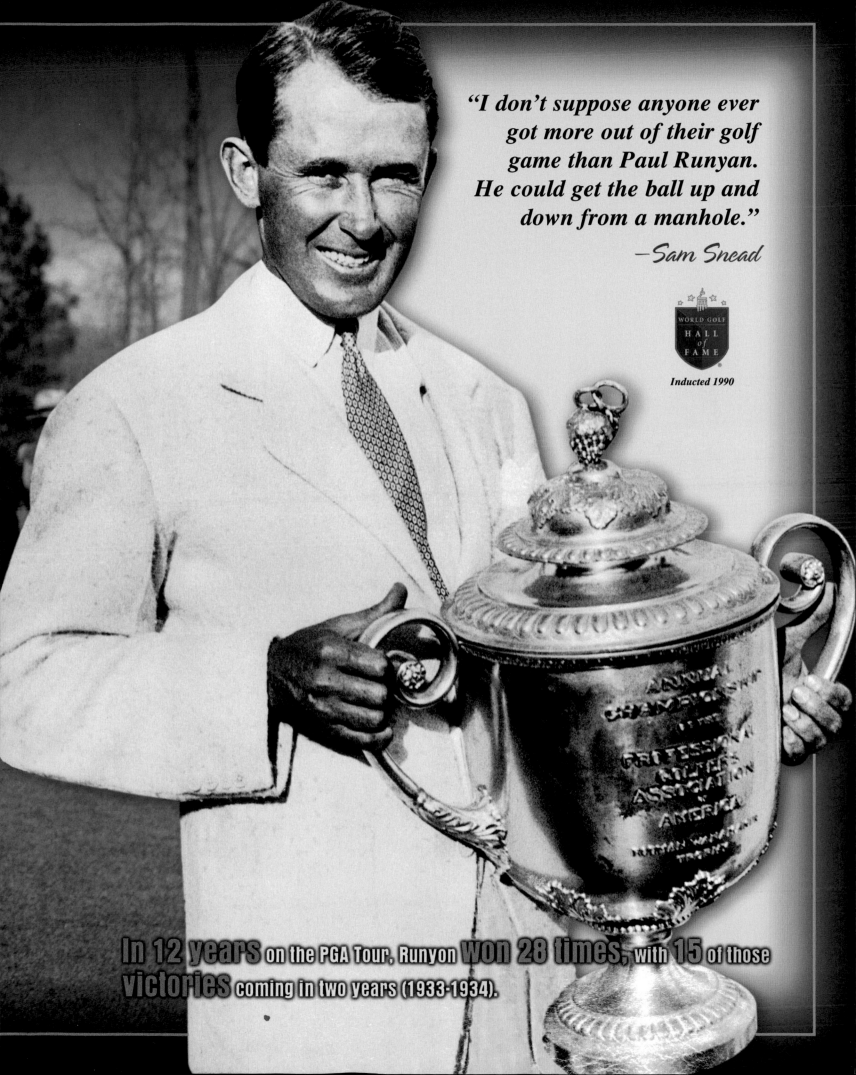

"I don't suppose anyone ever got more out of their golf game than Paul Runyan. He could get the ball up and down from a manhole."

—Sam Snead

WORLD GOLF HALL of FAME

Inducted 1990

In 12 years on the PGA Tour, Runyon won 28 times, with 15 of those victories coming in two years (1933-1934).

"The zone is the ability to give 110 percent of your attention and your focus to the shot. When I'm on the tee, I'll see a divot in the fairway and try to run my ball over the divot—and succeed. That's the zone."

—Nick Price

38

Nick
Price

Born: **January 28, 1957**
Durban, South Africa

24 international victories to go with his **17 Tour wins;** in the **1990s,** he and Tiger Woods tied for **most victories** on the PGA Tour with **15.**

There is no better dinner companion on the PGA Tour than the man with four names and three major titles. Affable, genuine and unassuming, Nicholas Raymond Leige Price collected his 17th PGA Tour victory at the 2002 MasterCard Colonial, 19 years after winning his first Tour event, the 1983 World Series of Golf.

Price won his first major, the PGA Championship, in 1992 at Bellerive Country Club in St. Louis, the same course where another South African-born golfer, Gary Player, captured his only U.S. Open in 1965. In 1994 at Turnberry's Ailsa Course, Price eagled the 16th

hole, birdied the 17th and parred the 18th to steal the British Open title from Swede Jesper Parnevik, who bogeyed the final hole and lost by a shot.

A native of South Africa but a citizen of Zimbabwe, Price cruised to a five-stroke lead with a second-round 65 in the 1994 PGA at Southern Hills and finished six shots ahead of runner-up Corey Pavin. He also shares the competitive course record at Augusta National with Greg Norman; Price shot 63 in the third round of the 1986 Masters.

Won **18 PGA Tour titles** and **two PGA Seniors Championships.**

Julius
BOROS

Born: March 3, 1920 Fairfield, Conn.
Died: May 28, 1994

39

"By the time you get to your ball, if you don't know what to do with it, try another sport."

— Julius Boros,
on not taking a practice swing
before every shot.

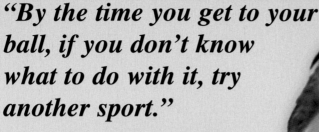

Inducted 1982

With a swing often compared to the smooth, slow movement of molasses, Julius Boros compiled an enviable record during his extended sojourn on the PGA Tour. Trained as an accountant, Boros did not turn pro until 1950, but he quickly made his mark. In 1952, he was the leading money-winner and player of the year on the Tour, thanks largely to a four-stroke victory over Porky Oliver in the U.S. Open.

Eleven years later, "Moose" would win his second Open title in a memorable playoff against Arnold Palmer and Jacky Cupit. Boros birdied two of the last three holes at The Country Club in

Brookline, Mass. to shoot 72 in the final round and tie Cupit and Palmer at 293 (nine over par). In the playoff, Boros used his extraordinary touch around the greens to one-putt 10 times en route to a 70. Cupit finished three shots back, and Palmer, who triple-bogeyed the par-four 11th hole, struggled to a 76.

In 1968, Boros became the oldest player ever to win a major, when at age 48 he beat Palmer and Bob Charles by one shot in the PGA Championship at Pecan Valley in San Antonio, Texas. He died in 1994, sitting in a golf cart near the 16th hole at Coral Ridge Country Club in Ft. Lauderdale.

The youngest player to win the British Open, at age 17, also the first golfer to record a hole-in-one in a major championship, and the only player to win four consecutive championships.

"Deeply regretted by numerous friends and all golfers, he thrice in succession won the championship belt and held it without rivalry and yet without envy, his many amiable golfing qualities being no less acknowledged than his golfing achievements."

— *Inscription on a plaque dedicated to Young Tom in St. Andrew's Cathedral.*

No story contains the polar extremes of triumph and dejection to a greater degree than that of Young Tom Morris. A golf professional at age 13, Young Tom succeeded his father, legendary Old Tom Morris, as British Open champion in 1868. His first-round score of 47 over Prestwick's 12-hole course is one of the greatest rounds ever played.

Young Tom repeated as champion in 1869 and 1870, winning by three and 12 shots, respectively, and retiring the Moroccan belt of red leather and silver that served as the championship trophy.

When the Open resumed in 1872, Young Tom managed a three-stroke victory over David Strath and was first to possess the Claret Jug that goes to the champion to this day.

Young Tom was playing an exhibition with his father at North Berwick on Sept. 11, 1875, when he learned that his wife of a year and son both had died during childbirth. The disconsolate golfer literally drank himself to death. Young Tom died on Christmas morning 1875 of a hemorrhage in his lung—but most said it was a broken heart that killed him.

Young Tom Morris

40

Born: **April 20, 1851 St. Andrews, Scotland**

Died: **December 25, 1875**

"He's No. 1 in the world. Probably should have beaten me on paper, but I gave him a good go. ... I'm looking forward to the next time."

—*Ernie Els,*

after losing to Tiger Woods in a playoff at the 2000 Mercedes Championships.

Nicknamed "Big Easy" as much for his tempo on the golf course as for his low-key personality, Ernie Els startled the golf establishment in 1994 when he became the first foreign-born player since David Graham in 1981 to win the U.S Open.

Els claimed the first of his two Open titles in a playoff that included Scotsman Colin Montgomerie and American Loren Roberts. Monty shot 78 and dropped out of the playoff after 18 holes on Monday, June 20, but Els and Roberts remained tied at 74. In only the second Open to go to sudden death since a 1953 rule change had provided for that possibility, Els triumphed with a birdie to Roberts' par at the second extra hole.

In 1997 at Congressional Country Club, Els placed his name on the U.S. Open trophy a second time with a one-shot victory over Montgomerie. In doing so, Els became the first foreign player since Scotland's Alex Smith (1906 and 1910) to win the Open twice. Els is also the only player ever to finished second in three straight majors in the same year (Masters, U.S. Open and British Open in 2000).

Els ended Tiger Woods' quest for the grand slam by winning the 2002 British Open at Muirfield.

Ernie Els

Born: October 17, 1969
Johannesburg, South Africa

41

Has **17 PGA Tour victories;** won at least one tournament per year from 1983 through 1989; **Captain of the 2001/2002 Ryder Cup team.**

Curtis Strange

Born: **January 30, 1955**
Norfolk, Va.

"You tend to get impatient with poor shots or less-than perfect shots, but you have to remember less-than perfect shots win Opens."

—*Curtis Strange*

Not since Ben Hogan had won back-to-back U.S. Open titles in 1950 and 1951 had anyone else won two straight, but Curtis Strange was on the verge of matching Hogan's feat as he played the final round of the 1989 Open at Oak Hill Country Club in Rochester, N.Y. Strange had thrust himself into contention with a brilliant 64 in the second round—a bogey at the 17th cost him a chance to tie Johnny Miller's single-round Open record of 63—but he backed up to the field with a 73 on Saturday.

Strange was all business in the final round. With a decisive birdie at the 16th hole, he came home in even-par 70 and won the championship by a stroke over Chip Beck, Mark McCumber

and Ian Woosnam—after third-round leader Tom Kite had self-destructed with a 78. Strange's 1989 victory followed his 1988 playoff victory over Nick Faldo at The Country Club in Brookline, Mass.

Strange was following the trail blazed by his father, Tom Strange Jr., a gifted Virginia amateur who later turned pro and tied for 48th place in the 1967 U.S. Open at Baltusrol before he lost his battle with cancer when Curtis was 14. Tom Strange won the inaugural Easter Amateur in 1957. Curtis followed his 1974 NCAA championship with a victory at the Eastern in 1975.

"I'm about five inches from being an outstanding golfer. That's the distance my left ear is from my right."

—Ben Crenshaw

Collected **19 Tour victories** during his career. In 1971 and 1973 he **won the NCAA individual golf championship.** In 1972 he shared it with University of Texas teammate Tom Kite.

Ben Crenshaw

Born: January 11, 1952
Austin, Texas

Winner of two Masters titles, the last in 1995, Ben Crenshaw returned to the national spotlight as captain of the Ryder Cup in 1999. Under his leadership the United States team rallied from a four-point deficit on the final day to reclaim the Cup from the European side. The U.S. clinched the match when Justin Leonard sank a 50-foot birdie putt on the 17th green to defeat Spain's Jose Maria Olazabal.

Crenshaw's victory at the 1995 Masters was every bit as emotional. One week after the death of his friend and teacher, Harvey Penick, Crenshaw posted a final round 68 at Augusta National to defeat Davis Love III by one stroke. Those around the 18th green witnessed a stirring scene, when Crenshaw holed his short, decisive putt and fell into the arms of his caddie, Carl Jackson, utterly spent.

Crenshaw's 1984 Masters victory, by two strokes over Tom Watson, included one of the tournament's enduring highlights—Crenshaw's timely birdie putt of at least 60 feet on the 10th green. Crenshaw survived on Tour with a swing that was technically flawed, but he made up for that deficiency with an extraordinary putting touch and an intense competitive fire.

45

"*A bad attitude is worse than a bad swing.*"

— *Payne Stewart*

11 PGA Tour wins, including his **three major championships.** He also posted **seven international victories,** among them the Indonesian Open, Indian Open and the Dutch Open.

The crash of a private jet in October of 1999 cut short Payne Stewart's career at its most successful juncture. In February of that year, Stewart had broken a four-year victory drought at the AT&T Pebble Beach National Pro-Am. In June, he won his third major championship by one stroke over Phil Mickelson in one of the most dramatic U.S. Opens ever played. Stewart holed a 15-foot par putt on the 72nd hole to secure the victory after Mickelson had narrowly missed a birdie from 35 feet.

In September, Stewart was an important part of the victorious American Ryder Cup team, which rallied from four points to win the Cup on the final day. His flight to Dallas on Oct. 25 was to be a routine business trip. Stewart was headed for Frisco, Texas, to look over the site of a golf course to be built for his alma mater, Southern Methodist University. But his plane lost pressure, veered off course and crashed near Aberdeen, S.D.

Known for his colorful outfits, which always included knickers during tournament competition, Stewart won his first major at Kemper Lakes Golf Club in Hawthorne Woods, Ill., where he edged Andy Bean, Mike Reid and Curtis Strange by one shot for the PGA Championship. He followed that victory with his first U.S. Open title in 1991, when he defeated Scott Simpson in an 18-hole playoff at Hazeltine National.

WORLD GOLF
HALL
of
FAME

Inducted 2001

Payne Stewart

Born: January 30, 1957 Springfield, Mo.
Died: October 25, 1999

"I thought I would never play golf again… and to me, to be right here standing in front of you with a green jacket, you know, it's some achievement."

—Jose Maria Olazabal, who overcame back problems to win the 1999 Masters.

46

Six victories on the PGA Tour, including **two majors** and **22 international wins.** Named to **seven Ryder Cup teams.**

Jose Maria Olazabal

Born: February 5, 1966
Fuenterrable, Spain

There's a serious side to Jose Maria Olazabal — and an intensely competitive one. Consider what happened at the 1999 U.S. Open at Pinehurst No. 2. Olazabal came to Open as reigning Masters champion with the feeling that Donald Ross' masterpiece in the North Carolina Sandhills might be a perfect fit for his extraordinary short game.

Far from completing the second leg of the Grand Slam, Olazabal shot five-over-par 75 in the first round. Frustrated by his failure to post a competitive score, Olazabal broke his hand against the wall of his hotel room and was forced to withdraw from the championship.

That same competitive desire, however, had stood "Chemma" in good stead in April, when his deft play around the greens ultimately left him two shots ahead of Davis Love III at Augusta National. In the 1994 Masters, Olazabal had beaten Tom Lehman by the same margin. Between his two Masters victories, Olazabal endured an 18-month absence from competition because of back problems.

21 PGA Tour wins, including two majors.
Member of three Ryder Cup teams.

"Fact is, I might do anything now because this is the happiest moment of my life."

—Craig Wood

After his breakthrough victory at the 1941 Masters.

In an era when nicknames seemed to be a competitive requirement, Craig Wood was known as the "Beltin' Blond." Legend has it that he launched a drive more than 400 yards—albeit wind-aided—at the 1933 British Open at St. Andrews.

No one would have faulted Wood if he had thought of himself as a victim. Like Greg Norman, Wood is better known for the majors he lost than for the two he won. He lost the 1933 British Open to Denny Shute in a playoff. In 1934 Paul Runyan beat Wood for the PGA Championship on the second hole of sudden death after their 36-hole final ended in a tie. At the 1935 masters, Wood was three-shots clear of Gene Sarazen in the final round—until the Squire holed out for double-eagle at 15. The next day, Sarazen won the title in a playoff.

After losing the 1939 U.S. Open to Byron Nelson in a playoff that required 36 holes, Wood might have despaired of winning a major. But in 1941 he captured the Masters by three shots over Nelson and followed that with a three-stroke victory over Shute in the 1941 U.S. Open at Colonial Country Club.

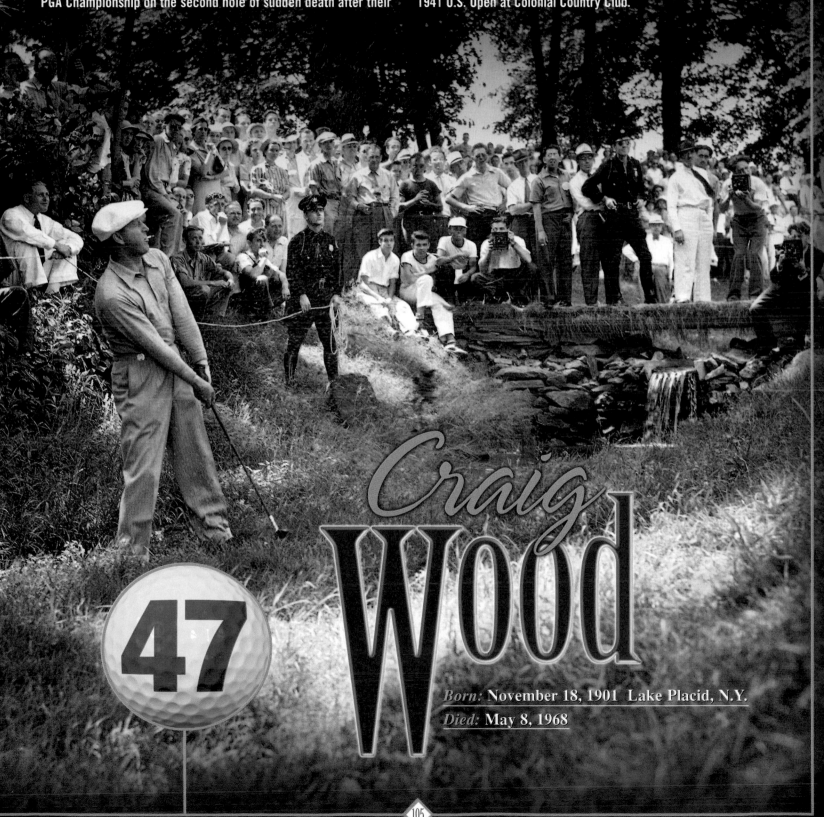

Craig
Wood

47

Born: November 18, 1901 Lake Placid, N.Y.
Died: May 8, 1968

4 major victories: **British Opens**
in 1861, 1862, 1864, 1867.

Old • Tom

Morris

Born: June 16, 1821   St. Andrews, Scotland
Died: May 24, 1908

48

Perhaps no one in the golf history has had as great and as varied an impact on the game as Old Tom Morris. From his shop beside the 18th hole at the Old Course—a fixture in St. Andrews to this day—Old Tom dispensed the clubs and balls he made, along with an ample supply of philosophy.

Morris won four of the first eight British Opens—the first in 1861, the last in 1867—all played at Prestwick. In 1868, his son, Young Tom, succeeded him as champion and claimed the title four straight times. Old Tom served as Custodian of the Links of St. Andrews from 1864–1902, but his most important legacy might well reside in the courses he designed.

A genius when it came to the routing of golf holes, Old Tom is credited with laying out Muirfield, the site of the 2002 Open, renowned Lahinch in Ireland and Royal Dornoch in northern Scotland, the training ground for the most prolific architect of all—Donald Ross.

"To generations of people all over the world his name and his picture epitomized the game."

—*James K. Robertson,*

from the book: St. Andrews, Home of Golf

"Every kid learning how to play golf dreams about winning the Masters, about winning the Open, not about being the leading money winner. I've never shortchanged myself on dreams."

— Tom Kite

Despite a successful PGA Tour career that has spanned more than three decades, despite a player-of-the-year performance and more than $1.3 million in prize money in 1989, Kite suffered under the uncomfortable designation "best player never to win a major" until his breakthrough U.S. Open victory at Pebble Beach in 1992.

As the championship unfolded, a triumph for Kite seemed improbable at best. Dr. Gil Morgan reached double figures under par for the first time in Open history during the third round and held a seven-shot lead at 12 under par with 29 holes remaining. But

Morgan blew sky-high with a 77-81 finish and slipped into a tie for 13th as Kite, Jeff Sluman and Colin Montgomerie battled for the title.

What turned out to be the decisive stroke came on the seventh hole in the final round, when Kite hooked a six iron left of the green into a gale blowing straight into his face off the Pacific Ocean. With bogey the likely result, Kite instead hole his pitch shot for birdie at the famous short par three and went on to edge Sluman by one shot and Montgomerie by two.

Through the mid-point of the 2002 season, Kite had added **five Senior PGA Tour victories** to his **19 wins on the PGA Tour.** Kite played on **seven Ryder Cup teams** and captained the 1997 squad.

Tom
Kite

Born: December 9, 1949
McKinney, Texas

49

13 PGA Tour victories, in only eight seasons including **one major,** the British Open in 2001. Holds the **record** for **lowest final round score,** shooting a **59** at the 1999 Bob Hope Chrysler Classic.

"You know, I beat them all this week and I played really good. It feels wonderful."

—David Duval,
after his first major victory.

In the 2001 British Open at Royal Lytham and St. Anne's, David Duval finally accomplished what others had expected of him for several years—he won his first major. With a 10-under-par total of 274, Duval finished three shots ahead of surprising Swede Niclas Fasth, who posted 277 long before the leaders finished and watched as every contender save Duval slid backwards. His victory in the British aside, Duval carved out a permanent niche in golf history with one of the greatest rounds ever played. In the final round of the 1999 Bob Hope Chrysler Classic, he eagled the 72nd hole (the 18th at PGA West's Arnold Palmer course) to shoot 59 and win the tournament by a stroke over Steve Pate. Duval's 59 matched identical scores recorded by Al Geiberger (1977) and Chip Beck (1991), but no one before Duval had ever shot 59 in the final round to win a Tour event.

A streaky player who has fought a variety of nagging injuries in recent years, Duval won the last three events of 1997, and in 1999 he was the first player to win four events before the Masters since Johnny Miller accomplished the feat in 1974. One thing is certain: Duval has excellent golf genes—his father Bob Duval is a member of the Senior PGA Tour.

David Duval

50

Born: **November 9, 1971**
Jacksonville, Fla.

Tiger's Tale

'He is the chosen one'

Tiger's No. 1, and he's only just begun

It was October 6, 1978, and Tiger Woods was about to make his first appearance on a nationally televised variety show.

He was a novelty. He was a prodigy. He was Mozart with a golf club. He was 2 years old.

Wearing khaki shorts, a white shirt with red trim and a bright red cap to match his bright red golf bag, Woods bounced onto the soundstage of the Mike Douglas Show, flashing a toddler's version of the disarming smile that remains a part of his repertoire to this day.

As comedian Bob Hope cracked jokes and actor Jimmy Stewart watched with amusement, Woods missed three putts of approximately four feet in length on a makeshift Astroturf green. Frustrated, Woods picked up the ball, placed it six inches from the flagstick and promptly knocked it into the hole.

Nearly 13 years later, Woods would win his first United States Golf Association national title, the 1991 Junior Amateur. In 1978, however, the notion of Tiger Woods as the winner of multiple major championships resided almost exclusively in the dreams and aspirations of his father, Earl Woods, and had not yet transferred from father to son.

Nevertheless, the precocious 2-year-old found a way to do what he has been doing ever since—devising a plan to get the ball into the hole, and executing the plan to perfection.

Less than two years into the 21st century, Woods stands at the pinnacle of his sport, or to be more accurate, at the pinnacle of all sport. Winner of eight major championships, youngest to win a career Grand Slam and the only player ever to hold all four professional major titles at the same time, Woods is the PGA Tour's all-time single-season and career money leader.

He has held golf's No. 1 world ranking for more than two years without interruption. More recognizable worldwide than the President of the United States,

Woods has supplanted his friend and basketball counterpart, Michael Jordan, as the world's most influential athlete.

Though Woods has curtailed his playing schedule in recent years as his focus has shifted more heavily toward golf's four major championships—The Masters, U.S. Open, British Open and PGA—his visibility hasn't suffered. Lucrative endorsement deals with Nike (with whom he signed a $40-million contract shortly after turning pro in 1996), Wheaties and Buick, to name a few, have kept his face—and his carefully orchestrated image—in the public eye.

When Woods chooses to play in a particular event on the PGA Tour, television ratings inevitably skyrocket, particularly when he occupies a spot at or near the top of the leaderboard. In fact, TV coverage of professional golf has drawn no small degree of criticism over the past few years—notably from other players on Tour—for concentrating on Woods (when he's not in contention) at the expense of tournament leaders with CDD (charisma deficit disorder).

There's a reason for Woods' popularity with the galleries and viewing audiences. To watch him in person or on television is to watch history being written. With every tournament, Woods adds to

Any questions about his personal life are as far out of bounds as a wild John Daly tee shot.

his legend. And with a regularity that thoroughly transcends mere happenstance, he will produce precisely the right shot at precisely the right moment, as though the force of his will can influence the results of his actions. In a word, he is fascinating, even spellbinding.

Yet the dichotomy of Woods is this: the most visible, recognizable and sought-after athlete in the world may also be the most isolated. Woods' handlers, who "simplify" his schedule and slow the flood of demand on his time to a trickle, rarely acquiesce to one-on-one interview requests. Woods himself, though quite affable in a pressroom setting, chooses his words as meticulously as he chooses the type of shot he plans to play on the golf course.

To a degree, that's understandable. Woods was shocked in March of 1997 when off-hand comments he made to reporter Charles Pierce in the back of a limousine—comments that included off-color jokes about African-Americans and lesbians—appeared verbatim in "Gentleman's Quarterly." The erosion of trust that stemmed from that experience has shaped Woods' attitude toward the media irrevocably.

Later that month, at the 1997 Tournament Players Championship in Florida, Woods was asked if the fallout from the GQ story would make him more

It is believed Ed "Fluff" Cowan, who carried Woods' bag during his record-setting win in the 1997 Masters, was fired in part because he was too friendly with the press.

cautious with the press.

"Very cautious with you guys, yes," he admitted, "because I have learned my lesson. I had to learn it the hard way. I have learned that some—I guess some writers have an agenda going into an article. Obviously, you guys do. But some more than others."

After a tournament round, Woods can describe every shot he hit that day to the nth detail. He will recall the specific swing mechanics that produced either the shot he expected or a shot that went awry. He can describe the minutiae of every stroke—the weather conditions, the wind, the direction the grass was growing.

But the player who maintained a list of Jack Nicklaus' major golf accomplishments in his room as a child reveals very little of himself, of what drives him. He speaks of short-term goals—playing the final round of the 2000 U.S. Open at Pebble Beach without a bogey, for instance—but is silent about his long-term

pursuit of Nicklaus' record 18 professional majors. He resolutely refuses to buy into talk of personal rivalries with his fellow competitors.

And questions about his personal life are as far out of bounds as a wild John Daly tee shot.

Nor are those in Woods' inner circle likely to come forth with any significant revelations. Woods' mother, Kultida, isn't talking. Neither are the women in Woods' life: ex-girlfriend Joanna Jagoda, now a law student in California, and current flame Elin Nordegren, a Swedish model who was working as a nanny for fellow PGA Tour pro Jesper Parnevik when Woods met her at the 2001 British Open.

Ed "Fluff" Cowan, the caddie with the Santa Claus smile, carried Woods' bag during his record-setting victory in the 1997 Masters. But Cowan liked to sign autographs, and he was friendly with the press. During the 18 months after his Masters win, Woods made significant changes to his game. One of them

was firing Cowan.

Fluff's replacement was New Zealander Steve Williams, who spent more than a decade on Raymond Floyd's bag. Williams doesn't do interviews that involve Tiger, and with good reason. Williams earns more money than the highest-paid player on New Zealand's legendary All Blacks national rugby team.

Butch Harmon, Woods' teacher and swing coach since 1993, is likewise mum when it comes to his protégé's personal life and feelings.

To get a fleshed-out picture of Woods, those who follow golf seriously or casually must depend on their own empirical observations and on the comments of others, particularly his fellow pros. But the result,

"It seems like we're not playing in the same ballpark right now. When he's on, you don't have much of a chance."

—Ernie Els

necessarily, is a portrait painted by a committee of impressionists.

"It wasn't that long ago that I said there would never be another Jack Nicklaus," Mark Calcavecchia said after one of Woods' dominating performances. "But we're looking at one. He is it. He is the chosen one."

After finishing tied for second with Miguel Angel Jimenez in the 2000 U.S. Open at Pebble Beach—15 shots behind Woods' record 12-under-par pace—South African Ernie Els could only shrug his shoulders.

"I don't know how much more there is to say about him," Els said. "We've talked about him for two years now, and I guess we're going to talk about him for the next three. Whatever I say is going to be an understatement. At the moment, he's just a great player.

"It seems like we're not playing in the same ballpark

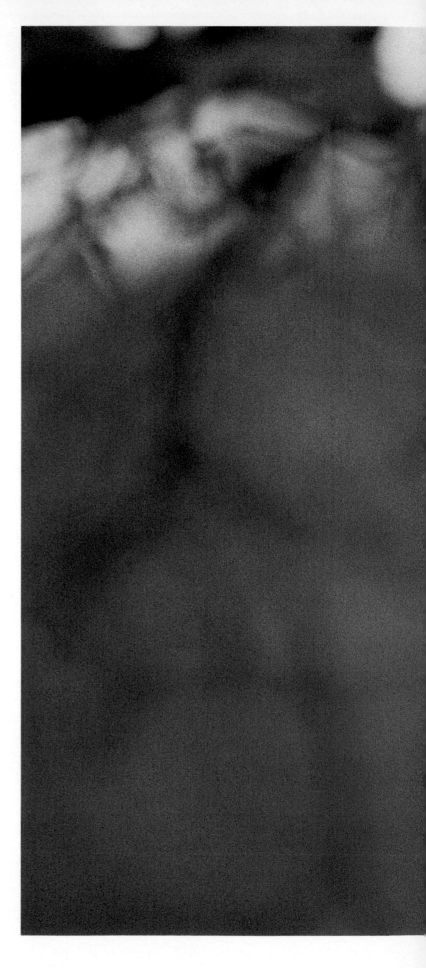

right now. When he's on, you don't have much of a chance. This week, myself, with my own game, I played one good round of golf. But still, I guess if I played out of my mind, I probably still would have lost by five, six or seven. He's a phenomenal player. That's an understatement, probably."

Athletes from other sports have taken note of Woods' extraordinary accomplishments. When Woods overcame a seven-stroke deficit to Matt Gogel on the final nine (including a hole-out for eagle at Pebble Beach's par-four 15th hole) to win his sixth straight tournament at the 2000 AT&T Pebble Beach National Pro-Am, NBA All-Star point guard Jason Kidd (then of the Phoenix Suns) was quoted on the subject in the Suns' e-mail newsletter, "In the Post."

"Tiger's en fuego," Kidd said. "He came out and played! I think people are starting to get intimidated by Tiger. If he's on the leaderboard, they know that at some point he's going to make a run at you. If he ever gets within a stroke or two, people feel the heat of Tiger and it showed yesterday. He just had an incredible final round and he's been doing it all year."

> *"He plays supernaturally."*
> — Tom Watson

Tom Watson and Thomas Bjorn put it more succinctly.

"He plays supernaturally," Watson observed.

"I certainly think someone out there is playing on a different planet than the rest of us," Bjorn said, after a second-place tie with Els in the 2000 British Open at St. Andrews—eight strokes behind Woods' record-setting 19-under-par 269 at the Old Course.

Eldrick T. Woods, however, is very much a product of Planet Earth. He was born to African-American Earl Woods, a lieutenant colonel in the Army, and Thailand native Kultida Woods on December 30, 1975, in Cypress, California. Woods was actually the second person Earl Woods nicknamed "Tiger." The

Before he turned pro, Tiger made a name for himself as a youngster on the national amateur scene. Here he tees off during the Pro-Am of the 1992 Los Angeles Open at Riviera Country Club.

first was Vuong Dang Phong, a South Vietnamese officer whom Earl admired for his bravery.

When Vietnam fell to Ho Chi Minh's forces in 1972, Earl Woods lost track of his Vietnamese friend, but he vowed to nickname his first child "Tiger." In 1975 he fulfilled that promise.

Tiger Woods began developing the athleticism that characterizes his own golf swing at a very early age. Earl Woods describes Tiger's first exposure to golf in the foreword he contributed to "A-Game" Golf, a book by John Anselmo, the gifted teaching pro who nurtured Woods well into his teens.

"When Tiger was an infant, he sat in a high chair and watched me hit shots into a net set up in the garage of our home," Earl Woods writes. "Every once in a while I would glance back out of the corner of my eye to check on Tiger, only to find him staring at

the club in my hands, his eyes big as marbles, waiting for me to make the next swing.

"It was very clear that Tiger was very curious about the mechanics of the swing and the ins and outs of what made my technique tick. Oh, boy, did he get excited when the club hit the ball powerfully into the net. Even back then I could see he was anxious to jump down from his perch and give golf a go.

"Little did I know that there would be such a short gap between the time Tiger first watched me hit balls and when he actually swung the club himself. To shorten a long story, when Tiger was ten months old he climbed down from his high chair and hit the ball into the net. All I could do was yell to my wife, 'Honey, get in here, look at this!' My wife and I were amazed—rather shocked—that Tiger had learned so much so fast about the golf swing."

Legends Ray Floyd, left, and Greg Norman get a taste of things to come as they watch the amateur Eldrick "Tiger" Woods tee off during a practice round before his first Masters appearance in 1995.

Before his third birthday, Woods had appeared not only on the Mike Douglas Show but also on CBS News. In 1981 he stole the show as a 5-year-old on "That's Incredible."

At age 3, Woods reportedly toured nine holes in 48 strokes at the Navy Golf Club in Cypress, Calif. There's an oft-repeated story, possibly apocryphal, that Woods overcame a racially motivated loss of playing privileges by beating the Navy Club pro, who spotted his young opponent one stroke per hole.

As an 8-year-old, Woods won his first significant title, the Optimist International Junior Championship in 1984. Over the next seven years, Woods would claim the title five more times in various age groups.

After winning the Junior Amateur in 1991 at age

15, the youngest player ever to do so, Woods backed it up the following year with another championship. No other player, before or since, has ever won more than one Junior Amateur title. The exclamation point came in 1993, when Woods won the Junior Am for the third straight time. In those three national junior events, Woods got a strong taste of close, intense competition; all three of his final matches went the distance, with the 1991 and 1993 championships each requiring one extra hole.

Of all of Woods' well-documented accomplishments, including seven of 11 major titles from the 1999 PGA through the 2002 U.S. Open, his three straight victories in the Junior Amateur might be the most impressive. Realistically, a junior player has a window of opportunity of no more than four to five

Woods wears his emotions on his sleeve, whether it's the fist-pumping joy he showed after tying his match with Steve Scott on the 35th hole of the 1996 U.S. Amateur championship …

years, at the outside, to accomplish that feat before aging out of the division.

By 1994, Tiger's name was well-known among those who followed golf, but only a relative handful of fans had seen him play. That all changed with the 1994 U.S. Amateur Championship at the TPC at Sawgrass in Ponte Vedra, Fla. In the final, Woods squared off against Trip Kuehne (whose brother Hank Kuehne would avenge the family honor by winning the Amateur in 1998).

At the 35th hole of the final match—the Stadium Course's intimidating short par-three 17th—Woods gave a national television audience a glimpse of the future. His approach shot narrowly found dry land, and standing near the wooden bulkhead that surrounds the island green, Woods, who had erased a five-hole deficit, lined up a birdie putt from the fringe that would almost certainly prove decisive if it fell.

As the putt hit bottom, Woods showed the world his emotional Jimmy Connors-style fist pump—and the world was hooked. The 18-year-old Woods became the youngest player ever to win the Amateur when he finished off Kuehne 2-up.

Coincidentally, the 17th at Sawgrass played a prominent role in another important Woods victory in 2001. In the third round of the Players Championship, Woods made up four shots on 36-hole leader Jerry Kelly. The key shot was a serpentine 60-foot birdie putt from the back of the 17th green. Woods pulled within two of Kelly after three rounds and ultimately won the title by one stroke over Vijay Singh, when Kelly faded on the final 18.

With a second straight Amateur Championship in 1995, and a third in 1996 in a thrilling, come-from-behind 38-hole match against Steve Scott, Woods became the only player in history to win three straight U.S. Amateur titles. Not even golf's greatest amateur, Bobby Jones, could lay claim to that distinction.

... or the frustration he shows when his game goes awry.

The 1996 final was a study in Woods' resilience and power of focus. Five holes down to Scott after the morning round, Woods sought help from Harmon during the lunch break. Early in the afternoon he cut into Scott's lead but still was two down with three to play. On the 34th hole, Woods used his superior length to his advantage and made birdie to cut Scott's lead in half. At the 35th hole, Woods holed a long birdie he felt he had to make to even the match he would later win on the second extra hole.

Asked if he was disappointed with his performance during the morning 18, Woods found another way to describe his feelings.

"I was not disappointed; I was very pissed," he explained. "Butch says I was hot. And I guess you

could call that disappointed, I don't know. But I was pretty angry at myself over the way I played because I knew what I had to do, and I just didn't have it. And I was just trying to figure it out with my golf swing, but it just wasn't there. And thank God Butch saw some things and I went out there and played well in the afternoon."

As has become his custom, Woods was able to channel his emotions toward a positive outcome.

In fact, in winning 33 events since turning pro in 1996, Woods has established an all-but-bulletproof reputation as the greatest front-runner in the history of the game. He has tasted victory each of the eight times he has held or shared the lead after 54 holes of a major championship. Through the 2002 U.S. Open at Bethpage State Park's Black Course, Woods had gone on to win 25 of the 27 PGA Tour events in which he was leading or tied for the lead entering the final round.

To Woods' way of looking at it, success engenders more success, particularly in the majors. And whether he admits it or not, his success intimidates the rest of the field.

To Woods' way of looking at it, success engenders more success, particularly in the majors. And whether he admits it or not, his success intimidates the rest of the field.

"I think if there is any type of feeling like that, I think it's just because of the fact that I've positioned myself there enough times on Sundays in my short career, and I've won," Woods said on Media Day for the 2001 PGA Championship. "I think I may have, I guess, got the reputation that I can play down the stretch. Especially when I've had the lead going into the final round, I've had a lot of success with the lead going into Sunday.

"I don't know if the players feel that way, but I know that because of my past experiences that I feel pretty good heading into Sunday if I'm near the lead.

"I would have to say that—the theory that Jack (Nicklaus) put out and has said for countless years—playing major championships is probably the smallest field you play in all year long because of the conditions. And the fact that what tournament it is, guys are talking about it, thinking about it; it's a major championship, and I think they might put added pressure on themselves. I think if I can play well—I've proven to myself that I can win the major championships, and I think that eases things and allows me to go on and win others.

"Because of what tournament it is and the course setup, and I guess the whole climate that week, I think that puts so much pressure on the guys that they start thinking about a lot of things, other than just actually going out there and hitting golf shots."

That's certainly been the case in most of Tiger's major championship victories, dating to his first Masters win in 1997. Scotsman Colin Montgomerie, who has never won in the United States, trailed Woods by three shots after 36 holes. Montgomerie happened to mention that he looked forward to going head-to-head with Woods in the third round.

Monty finished 74-81 and plummeted into a tie for 30th place, as Woods beat Tom Kite for the title by a record 12 shots.

In the 2000 U.S. Open, Woods turned in perhaps the most dominating performance in major championship history. He finished 12 under par at Pebble Beach—the only time a player has achieved double digits under par in a U.S. Open—to defeat Els and Jimenez by a record 15 shots. Els was paired with Woods for the final round but was just along for the ride—and knew it.

"He dominated from day one," Els said after the final round. "From the first hole, he started dominating and never let go. I had the privilege to play with him today. I saw the weather before we went out, and I knew I had no chance. I tried to play a solid round of golf, which I did from tee to green, but I didn't make too many putts. My thoughts about Tiger: he didn't miss too many shots. I only saw him miss one putt. And he got it up-and-down every time he missed the green. When you have a guy playing like that, you have no chance.

"If I could play like that, like he just did the last four days in a major championship, that would be my ultimate golfing week. It seems like—it's tough to comment on it. He just played a perfect U.S. Open this week. He did nothing wrong. And that's kind of what keeps him ahead. When you're a little kid, 4 or 5 years old, and dream about winning championships and running away from the field, that's kind of how you have to play."

Els wasn't as gracious at the 2000 British Open, and understandably so. Though he held the first-round lead, the pressroom buzzed with Tiger's attempt to complete the career Grand Slam at age 24.

"Shall I start talking about Tiger again?" Els snapped. "Jeez. No, not right now, no. Guys, that's a little unfair. I just shot 66. Talk about my round or get on the phone."

Ultimately, Els would tie for second, eight shots back.

But Woods didn't dominate every major he won in 2000. In the PGA Championship at Valhalla, unheralded journeyman Bob May matched the world's No. 1

There's little argument among players and pundits alike that Woods has a decided edge over the rest of the world. But why? The consensus is that he possesses perhaps the strongest mental game in the history of golf.

player birdie-for-birdie down the stretch, forcing Woods to hole a difficult downhill five-foot slider on the 72nd green to necessitate extra holes. Woods, of course, beat May by a shot in a three-hole playoff.

Most frequently victimized by Tiger's phenomenal powers of concentration has been Phil Mickelson, who has finished second or third eight times in majors without winning one. Mickelson chased Woods throughout the 2002 U.S. Open at the Black Course and fell short. Each time Mickelson narrowed Woods' advantage to two shots, Woods responded.

In an otherwise indifferent third round, for instance, Woods regained breathing room with a birdie at the Black's ultra-difficult 15th hole and followed with a deuce at the long par-three 17th. The four-stroke lead that resulted gave Woods enough margin to survive three-putts at the first two greens on Sunday, when he was paired with Sergio Garcia and shot 72 to Garcia's 74.

"It's difficult to compete with a player of Tiger's caliber, but I've been able to do it the last year or two," a bemused Mickelson said after the final round. "I haven't been able to really win as much as I would like, but I'm closer. And certainly I need to lower my score that I set. Heading in, I thought even par would be an incredible score for four rounds. I was able to accomplish that. I have to raise that if I'm going to win tournaments with Tiger in the field."

There's little argument among players and pundits alike that Woods has a decided edge over the rest of the world. But why? The consensus is that he possesses perhaps the strongest mental game in the

Where Tiger goes, so goes the crowds, whether flocking to TVs to watch tournaments or catching him on the course.

history of golf. As a junior player he began working with sport psychologist Jay Brunza on visualization techniques.

"I think Tiger Woods is the smartest golfer who ever played the game," says Augusta National member Johnny Harris, President of Quail Hollow Country Club in Charlotte, N.C.

Harris can get a seconding opinion from none other than Jack Nicklaus.

"He's very smart," Nicklaus said. "He understands the game and how to play it. In fact, I don't think you need to be a mental giant to play the game of golf. You have to have a little common sense. Tiger plays well within himself. He just does what he has to do

when he has to do it. That, to me, is how you play any sport. It's common sense, intelligent play, thinking out what you have to do and doing it. He has the ability to control himself to do it."

Nicklaus, who rarely watches golf on television, tuned in for the final nine holes of the 2002 Masters and couldn't believe his eyes. With Woods playing a steady, if unspectacular round, his challengers—Els and Singh in particular—hit the self-destruct button.

"Tiger played a good, intelligent back nine," Nicklaus said. "What did he shoot? Thirty-Seven the last nine holes to win the Masters? He didn't have to do anything else. He just played a good, solid, intelligent nine. If he were pressed, I think he would have shot a better nine.

"The guys self-destructed, one right after the other. I was sitting there watching it on television, and I said, 'Oh, my God, look at the shot he's trying to play.' Boom—write him off. 'Look at the shot he's trying to play!' Boom—write him off."

Nicklaus would be the first to buy into Woods' con-servative approach of playing each tournament in its turn, shot-for-shot, as banal as that might sound. But he doesn't believe that Woods, for lack of better competition, has set his sights on the Nicklaus record as his primary opponent.

"He'd better play against the tournament and the course first," Nicklaus said. "Then he can play against my records. I think Tiger, from an intelligence standpoint, knows you can't go out with a goal of playing against somebody's records as it relates to how you're playing. Sure, that may be his ultimate goal, to break my records, but when he's going out to play, he's going out to do the best he can shot-for-shot and hole-for-hole to produce the best score, which wins the golf tournament.

"The other guys are saying, 'This guy must be infallible. He doesn't make any mistakes.' But if they go back and look at it, they're the ones who are making the mistakes. I haven't seen anybody come around and shoot 34 or 35 or 33 on the last nine holes against him when they've had a chance to do so."

Perhaps that's because Woods' competitors feel the extra pressure of trying to match him shot-for-shot. As Mickelson explains it, Woods isn't likely to come back to the field when he's leading a major. It simply hasn't happened.

"I think the thing about Tiger is that he's the only leader that you don't have the hope that he'll falter," Mickelson said after his third-place finish at the 2002 Masters. "When other guys are up there, you know that if you can just stay around there, there's a good chance they might come back two or three shots, but Tiger doesn't ever seem to do that. So with that being the case, you know that you have to go after him to

> *"I think the thing about Tiger is that he's the only leader that you don't have the hope that he'll falter."*
>
> *— Phil Mickelson*

make birdies to catch him, which is why I think we saw guys taking aggressive plays and making bogeys and doubles because of it."

As committed as Woods is to the major championships, it's no surprise that he has developed a thorough understanding of what it takes to win—patience, focus and self-control.

"To win a major championship, it's a different thought process and a different understanding of the game," he says. "Most majors you're going to have to go out there and understand that par is a wonderful score. And that's the way the golf course is set up—to make sure that par is a good score. Most Tour events, you go out there and shoot four or five under, and you're probably four or five behind. That's the frustrating thing about playing Tour events. Guys get off to such quick starts.

"Look how many times in the past two years guys have been 17 under par for two rounds. That doesn't happen in a major. That's a credit to how the golf course is set up. It brings out the best in players. Guys who can strike the ball the best, keep their emotions in check and make the big putts—they're going to be right up at the top. You tend to see that it's always the same players time and time again, because those are the guys who understand their game and their emotions."

Remarkably, Woods' own personal highlight reel from the 2000 season, when he finished a combined 53 under par in the majors and won three of them, contains only one shot he would characterize as "perfect"—a 3 wood to the 14th green at the Old Course in the third round of the British Open.

"From a tight lie I had to hit a little draw into a left-to-right wind and carry the ball about 260 yards to a green guarded by a couple of nasty pot bunkers," Woods writes in "How I Play Golf," the instruction book he authored with the editors of "Golf Digest." "As with every shot I attempt, I visualized the ball's flight and how it should respond upon landing.

"Because it was a blind shot, I picked a crane in the distance as my target. The ball never left that line, and the shot turned out exactly as I had planned. Moments like that stay fresh in my mind, providing a positive image for future reference. Those images are critical when the game is on. They may even be the difference between success and failure."

What will happen if Woods manages to hit two or three or even four perfect shots during a single year on the Tour?

Nick Faldo, a former world No. 1 and the owner of six major titles, doubtless would prefer not to think about it.

"Tiger will be playing blindfolded by the year 2005 at our request. We'll buy him one," Faldo says.

Implied in Faldo's words is an acknowledgement that he and the rest of the players on Tour will be battling not just Tiger Woods the golfer, but the larger-than-life juggernaut his opponents have allowed him to become.

In his own quiet way, Woods will allow the apprehensions of his colleagues to work against them, just as Nicklaus did during his heyday. But Woods himself laughs at the notion that he has some sort of special mojo working on his behalf, even if Watson does describe his play as "supernatural."

"I don't know if I even have an aura, man," Woods once replied to a question that bordered on silly. "I just try to win."

> *"I don't know if I even have an aura, man," Woods once replied to a question that bordered on silly. "I just try to win."*

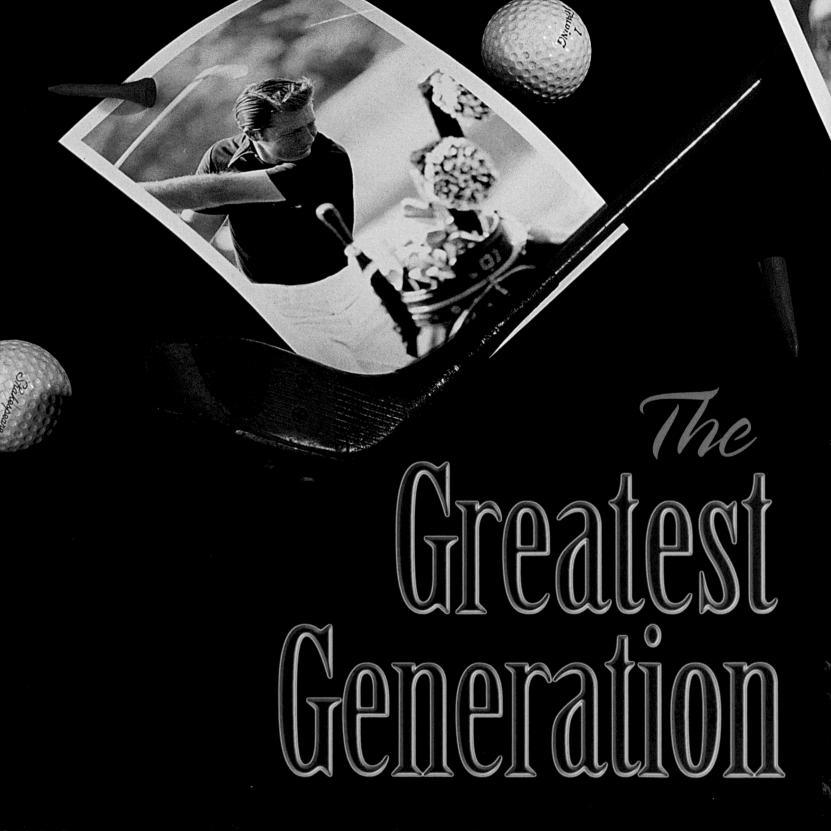

The
Greatest
Generation

Golf's golden era

Intense rivalries invigorated the game

Amid considerable fanfare—and a brief controversy —golf's greatest generation formally announced its arrival on Sunday, April 6, 1958.

It was in 1958 that golf writer Herbert Warren Wind first christened the 11th, 12th and 13th holes at Augusta National Golf Club "Amen Corner," and it was on that stretch of holes that Arnold Palmer began to define his legend.

Heavy rains had soaked Augusta National during the days leading up to the final round of The Masters, but at that time, the "imbedded ball rule" was not yet part of the United States Golf Association's "Rules of Golf." Instead, the tournament committee at The Masters had adopted a local rule allowing competitors to lift, clean and drop a ball that plugged in its own pitch mark.

Palmer, seeking his first professional major championship, came to Augusta's beautiful—and diabolical—par-three 12th hole with a one-stroke lead. But, as Palmer recounts in his book, "Playing By The Rules," his adrenaline-aided tee shot carried beyond the putting surface and imbedded in the fringe.

When Palmer saw his predicament, he summoned a rules official, who stubbornly (and incorrectly) refused to let the tournament leader remove the ball from its pitch mark. Over the continuing objections of the rules official, Palmer exercised another option, one that's available to any golfer when a ruling is in question—he played two balls, announcing his intention to count the second, if allowed.

Palmer chopped his original tee shot out of the turf and barely moved it. A chip and two putts later, he recorded a double-bogey 5 with the first ball. He then returned to the location of his tee shot, dropped a second ball, chipped close and saved par. But it was the

They did then and they do now: Arnie's Army still comes out to see Palmer tee it up today, 35 years past his prime.

5 that was posted on Augusta's scoreboards, for fans and fellow competitors alike to see.

Believing the tournament committee would rule in his favor, Palmer strode to the tee at the reachable par-five 13th and pounded a driver to the middle of the fairway. As he walked toward his ball, he noticed tournament founder Bobby Jones, America's most celebrated amateur golfer during his heyday, in the Roaring Twenties, observing the proceedings from his golf cart.

Under Jones' watchful eye, Palmer pulled a 3 wood and nailed it. His ball came to rest near the back of the treacherous green, 20 feet from the flagstick. An enormous roar from the gallery, which included a large number of early inductees into "Arnie's Army," accompanied Palmer's successful eagle putt.

So focused was Palmer on winning his first Masters that he quickly put the controversy at the

Arnold Palmer would win four Masters, the first of which came after some on-course controversy in 1958.

12th behind him.

"The fact is that I never felt that I was even remotely close to being wrong in my feelings about the ruling," Palmer says. "I think the thing was, I was so concerned about winning the golf tournament that I was just getting on with my business. And of course, the thing that no question helped inspire me was the fact that Bob Jones was watching everything that happened. He was in a golf cart following me that day and saw me play 12 and saw me play 13."

Palmer made par at the 14th but didn't learn of the tournament committee's decision on the events at the 12th until after he hit his drive at the par-five 15th. Tournament chairman John Winters delivered the news in person.

"I was walking down 15 when John Winters came out into the fairway to tell me what the committee had ruled," Palmer says. "And that's the first time I really got concerned. I thought, 'Ooh, suppose they ruled against me?' But as soon as I got close enough to him, I saw ... I don't know what you'd call it ... a satisfied look on his face, which encouraged me to think that I was right. He was not one to make a big issue out of it. He said, 'Mr. Palmer, the committee has ruled that you were right.' And that was it."

The double-bogey on the 12th hole was replaced with a 3 on the scoreboard, and Palmer went on to post a four-round total of 284, four under par. Both Fred Hawkins and Doug Ford missed putts to tie on the 72nd hole, and Palmer had his first major title.

Palmer would win The Masters three more times, in the even-numbered years from 1960 through 1964. After losing the 1960 British Open by one shot to Kel Nagle, Palmer claimed the Claret Jug the following two years, at Royal Birkdale and at Troon. In 1960, he won his only U.S. Open title at Cherry Hills Country Club in Denver with a final-round rally that established the "Arnold Palmer charge" as a commonplace in the sports idiom of the day.

"Gary (Player) is one of the greatest competitors I ever played against."

—Arnold Palmer

captured the first of his major championships, the British Open, in 1959, beating Fred Bullock and Flory Van Donck by two shots at Muirfield.

Though Player accumulated just 21 victories on the PGA Tour to Palmer's 60, the 5-foot-7, 150-pound Black Knight from Johannesburg (so named for his all-black outfits) won more than 125 times internationally and notched nine majors to Palmer's seven. Player is one of only five golfers to complete the professional career Grand Slam (the others being Gene Sarazen, Ben Hogan, Jack Nicklaus and Tiger Woods).

"Gary is one of the greatest competitors I ever played against," Palmer says of his former partner on the TV show Challenge Golf. "He wasn't the best player by far, but he was certainly one of the most competitive people that I've ever played against."

And then there was Nicklaus. When he arrived on the scene at the 1960 U.S. Open and finished second to Palmer as an amateur, Nicklaus began a rapid ascent to

But Palmer was far from the only golfer making a reputation for himself in the late '50s and early '60s, arguably the greatest generation that golf has seen. South African Gary Player, a fanatic about physical fitness long before weight training and conditioning were accepted practices among professional golfers,

the pinnacle of his sport and soon established himself as Palmer's most formidable rival. But Nicklaus, in the early days, wasn't yet the Golden Bear, despite the two U.S. Amateur titles and one NCAA championship that were already part of his resume. In fact, Palmer resorted to some good-natured needling in the

Jack Nicklaus (opposite) and The Black Knight, Gary Player, are two of only five golfers to have completed a career Grand Slam.

Tom Weiskopf (left) and Julius Boros would occasionally challenge the "Big Three," part of what made it the greatest generation, but they never enjoyed the success of Palmer, Player or Nicklaus.

press when he told golf fans they'd better watch out for "the fat boy" on the eve of the 1962 U.S. Open at Oakmont.

Of course, "the fat boy" defeated Palmer for the title in an 18-hole playoff. That was the first of Nicklaus' unprecedented 18 professional majors. By the middle of 1967, Nicklaus already had three Masters, two U.S. Opens, a British Open and a PGA Championship to his credit. In 1966, he became the first player to win back-to-back Masters on the way to a record six titles.

Palmer, Player and Nicklaus were all but inseparable in the minds of golf fans in the 1960s. They were the "Big Three," the second Great Triumvirate (inheriting the latter name from Harry Vardon, J.H. Taylor and James Braid, who ruled competitive golf during the years immediately before and after the

turn of the century).

The Big Three, however, weren't alone at the top of the pyramid. Julius Boros was quietly building his own championship record, including the 1968 PGA Championship at age 48, making him the oldest player ever to win a major. Billy Casper, who won three majors and 51 PGA Tour events, briefly supplanted Nicklaus as the arch-nemesis to Palmer, when he rallied from seven shots back with nine holes to play to "steal" the 1966 U.S. Open title from the King at the Olympic Club.

Gene "The Machine" Littler shot 68 in the final round of the 1961 U.S. Open at Oakland Hills Country Club in Birmingham, Mich., to snatch the trophy from Bob Goalby and hard-luck Doug Sanders, the most flamboyant golfer of the era but a man doomed all too often to runner-up finishes in the majors. Sanders could share his frustrations with temperamental Tom Weiskopf, who played in Nicklaus' giant shadow at Ohio State and on the PGA Tour.

According to Palmer, Weiskopf had "one of the great swings in the game, but I think he hurt himself with his attitude. He should have been far greater than he was."

Lee Trevino, who seldom did anything quietly, made an emphatic debut on the PGA Tour when he chose the 1968 U.S. Open at Oak Hill Country Club to register his first victory. Not only did Trevino defeat Nicklaus by four shots, but he also matched Nicklaus' U.S. Open record total of 275, which the Golden Bear had posted a year earlier in beating Palmer by four strokes at Baltusrol.

If any player proved a constant antagonist to Nicklaus, it was Trevino.

If any player proved a constant antagonist to Nicklaus, it was Trevino. On the first tee at Merion in 1971, moments before he and Nicklaus were to begin an 18-hole playoff for the U.S. Open title, Trevino dangled a rubber snake from the end of one of his clubs. The Merry Mex shot 68 to Nicklaus' 71 to claim his second U.S. Open championship.

A year later, Trevino chipped in for par from behind

the 17th green at Muirfield in the final round of the British Open. That shot gave Trevino a one-stroke victory in what Nicklaus still considers one of the two most disappointing moments of his career.

"If I had won that one, I would have held all four of them (major titles) at the same time," Nicklaus says. (Because of a scheduling quirk, Nicklaus won the 1971 PGA Championship in February at PGA National in Palm Beach Gardens, Fla. Though he did not win the subsequent Masters, U.S. Open or British Open in 1971, Nicklaus still held the PGA title when he won the Masters and U.S. Open in 1972.)

The early 1970s brought new tests for Nicklaus in the form of Johnny Miller, Tom Watson and Raymond Floyd. Miller was like a brilliant flash of light. He won the 1973 U.S. Open at Oakmont with a record 63 in the final round, and for two years thereafter he played like a virtuoso. But Miller's ascendance effectively ended with his British Open Championship in

1976 at Royal Birkdale, where he finished six shots clear of Nicklaus and young Seve Ballesteros.

Watson, on the other hand, had staying power. He won his first British Open title at Carnoustie in 1975, rallying to tie bon vivant Jack Newton at 279, then defeating Newton by a stroke in an 18-hole playoff. Two years later, Watson took the measure of Nicklaus in the "Duel in the Sun," where the two battled shot for shot until Watson assumed the lead for good on the 71st hole.

With British Open titles in 1980, 1982 and 1983 to go with Masters victories in 1977 and 1981 and a U.S Open win at Pebble Beach in 1982 (Nicklaus' other major disappointment), Watson established himself as a star of the highest magnitude.

Floyd, who liked to party and play golf for high stakes when not competing in PGA Tour events, finished his career with four majors—the 1976 Masters

The early '70s brought
new challengers to
Nicklaus and the rest
of the greatest gener-
ation, including
(counter clockwise,
from top left): Tom
Watson, Johnny Miller
and Ray Floyd.

Other legends from other eras include Francis Ouimet, center, shaking hands with Harry Vardon, left, and Ted Ray, at the 1913 U.S. Open. Below are (from left) Bobby Jones, Walter Hagen and Gene Sarazen in 1928.

with a record-tying score of 271 (broken by Woods with 270 in 1997), the 1986 U.S. Open at Shinnecock Hills, and the 1969 and 1982 PGA Championships. Still a factor well into his 40s, Floyd took Nick Faldo to a playoff before losing the 1990 Masters.

A generation spans roughly 25 years, but Golf's Greatest Generation lasted a few years longer than that, if only because Nicklaus, like Floyd, was able to stay competitive into his late 40s. Palmer was the first of the Big Three to win a major (1958), and Nicklaus was the last (1986). Between 1958 and 1986 inclusive, the names of Palmer, Player and Nicklaus were engraved on golf's most coveted trophies a total of 34 times.

But does that automatically qualify the Palmer/Player/Nicklaus generation—which includes a large cast of supporting characters—as the greatest in the history of the game? What about the era of the first Great Triumvirate, Vardon, Taylor and Braid? Did they not dominate the game even more thoroughly than the Big Three? Collectively, did they not win 16 of the 21 British Opens played from 1894 through 1914, after which World War I brought a five-year hiatus?

Perhaps so, but other than a few players such as Harold Hilton, Ted Ray, Alexander Herd and Jack White, the first Great Triumvirate was sadly lacking in "quality opposition."

If not Vardon, Taylor and Braid, what about golf's golden age in the Roaring Twenties and beyond? Walter Hagen was winning four straight PGA Championships while raising the level of respect accorded to professional golf exponentially. Gene Sarazen was completing the career Grand Slam—and making history in the process with his incredible double eagle at the 1935 Masters. Bobby Jones was winning the "impregnable quadrilateral," the four majors of his day, while the world lionized his accomplishments. And Francis Ouimet, who brought golf to the forefront of American consciousness with his U.S. Open victory in 1913, still had sufficient skill to win his second U.S Amateur title in 1931.

It's true that during the first decades of the 20th century, golf evolved from a provincial to an international game, but the depth of talent simply wasn't

The 1955 U.S. Open was the site where another great era of golfers convened: (from left) Ben Hogan, Sam Snead, Cary Middlecoff and Byron Nelson walk away from a practice round at the Olympic Club in San Francisco.

there. And after Jones' retirement from competitive golf at age 28 (after the Grand Slam of 1930), golf suffered through a sometimes uneasy transition from a predominantly amateur to a predominantly professional game, until Sam Snead, Byron Nelson and Hogan established themselves as bonafide stars.

But Snead, Nelson and Hogan can't be considered an "era" unto themselves. Though Snead won the first of his record 81 PGA Tour events in 1936 and the last in 1965, he lost four chances at the U.S. Open—the major title that eluded him—during what could

Jack Nicklaus (left), Sam Snead and Arnold Palmer get together at the 1962 British Open.

have been his most productive years. Because of the United States' involvement in World War II, the USGA did not hold Open championships from 1942-1945.

Exempt from military service for medical reasons, Nelson won 11 straight events in 1945 and 18 overall, but he retired from full-time competitive golf in 1946, two months after a disappointing playoff loss to Lloyd Mangrum in the U.S. Open. Coincidentally, 1946 was the year Hogan won his first major championship, the PGA.

In fact, Hogan might well have been a force in the

Palmer/Player/Nicklaus generation had he not developed an incurable case of the "yips," a maddening affliction that turns even short putts into agonizing uncertainties. From a ball-striking standpoint, Hogan remained competitive well into the 1960s.

If a lack of depth of talent and competition is enough to disqualify several generations before the advent of the Big Three, what about the current crop of players? From the zenith of the modern PGA Tour (Tiger Woods) to the lowliest player on the BUY.COM Tour, there has never been an assemblage of professional golfers so talent-rich.

There is, however, a fundamental difference between the days of the Big Three and the Tiger-versus-the-rest-of-the-world era. When Woods turned pro in 1996, he stepped into a vaccum. That's not to say players in the mid-1990s weren't talented. There simply weren't many viable players with extensive, established records in the major championships.

Those who had been major players, for one reason or another, had been relegated to the sidelines, or so it seemed. Ballesteros had fallen victim to back problems.

Nick Faldo, with six majors, was nearing 40, and after his 1996 Masters victory, the player who had been No. 1 in the world gradually slipped to No. 176. Greg Norman had already reached 40, and his devastating collapse in the final round of the 1996 Masters marked what may have been the end of his career as a major championship contender. The once bold putting stroke of the 46-year-old Watson had become tentative.

That left Nick Price, also closing in on 40 in 1996, as the only other everyday Tour player with more than two major titles. And in the last four years of the 1990s, Woods tied Price for most victories in the decade with 15.

Nicklaus believes Woods' ability to establish a championship record within a few years of turning pro is what sets him apart and enables him to dominate the game. Palmer, Player and Nicklaus all won multiple majors early in their respective careers, and instead of one dominant player emerging at the expense of all others, rivalries developed that invigorated the game.

"There are more good players today than when I was playing," Nicklaus says categorically. "But there

> *"There are more good players today than when I was playing, but there are fewer players who have a championship record, who have learned how to win championships."*
>
> —*Jack Nicklaus*

Jack Nicklaus believes Tiger Woods' emergence as a pro, coinciding with the fall of several veteran champions such as Greg Norman (above) and Nick Faldo (above, right), helped Woods establish a championship record within a few years of turning pro—setting him apart and enabling him to dominate the game.

are fewer players who have a championship record, who have learned how to win championships. Palmer won what? Seven majors? Player nine or eight (nine). Watson's won about eight. Trevino's won about eight (actually six). Those guys knew how to win. If I stumbled, they were there.

"The guys today (Tiger's) playing against, they're not bad players—they're good players. But they haven't had the experience of winning yet. Somebody's gonna have that. I keep saying that somebody's gonna come along. These guys today, give 'em a chance. They may not be there yet. Mickelson's a terrific player. As soon as Mickelson breaks through and wins one or two majors, he'll be a force to reckon with every time.

"But right now, I'm not sure he believes that he can win. You've got to believe in your head that you can win. You've got to have the experience of doing it. The hardest one to win is that first one, and then you follow it up and move from there. That's not easy. One of the reasons today why it's not as easy, you've got more competition from guys in that same boat. You've also got Tiger, too."

It was the rivalries of the '60s and '70s, combined with the personalities of the players, that rendered the participants of Golf Greatest Generation larger than life. Magnified by television as golf benefited from increased broadcast exposure—thanks largely to Palmer's charismatic presence—players approached their sport with bravado.

When Palmer asked sportswriter Bob Drum, "What would a 65 do?" during the break between the third and fourth rounds of the 1960 U.S. Open, it wasn't an idle question.

"I felt like I had played well enough that I should have been a lot better to start with than I was, and I

Because Nicklaus, Palmer and Player and all won multiple majors early in their careers, rivalries developed that invigorated the game.

felt like I could shoot 65, no question about it," Palmer says.

Drum's derisive reply, to the effect that "It wouldn't do you any good; you're too far back," only fueled Palmer's resolve. He drove the green at the par-four first hole, birdied six of the first seven holes, finished with 65 and won the championship by two strokes

While Palmer brought his "army" to the greens, Player was the Black Knight who worked best under pressure.

But Nicklaus was nothing if not focused (he was a pioneer in visualization techniques) and was not one to succumb to the distractions. When Nicklaus was asked about the relatively raucous crowds at the 2002 U.S. Open at Bethpage State Park in New York, he laughed.

"You're talking about New York. New York's always loud," Nicklaus says. "When I went around in '80 and won (the U.S. Open) at Baltusrol, every hole going from green to tee, people were smacking me on the back. I was trying to keep from getting hurt going to the next hole. It was great. It was fun. And that's what they said about Bethpage, right? I don't think that's changed any, and I don't think that's a big issue. It's bringing more people into the game, that's all."

Palmer, particularly, but Nicklaus and Player, too, all amplified the public's interest in golf, both from a spectator and a participation standpoint. Part of the attraction had to do with style. Player was the gritty Black Knight, who overcame his lack of length off the tee with adroit play around the greens. He is generally acknowledged as the greatest sand player of his day.

Nicklaus, though not the longest hitter of the era when compared to George Bayer or Mike Souchak, was nevertheless the longest hitter who had full command of the other elements of the game. Most of Nicklaus' contemporaries admitted they would pick the Golden Bear as most likely to make a five-foot putt, if his life depended on it.

And Palmer, with his relentlessly aggressive style, exhilarated his galleries, and broke their hearts. The loss to Player in the 1961 Masters—when Palmer needed par to win and double-bogeyed the 72nd hole—was hard enough to take. But the 1966 U.S. Open was cause for mourning.

In uncharacteristic fashion, with nine holes to play, Palmer had conceded the championship—to himself. Leading Billy Casper by seven shots at the turn, Palmer soon shifted his focus from winning the tournament to breaking Ben Hogan's then-record 276 total score, the lowest ever shot in the U.S. Open. As

Watson (center) who won numerous majors in the 1970s and 1980s, enjoyed his duels with Nicklaus.

Palmer pursued Hogan and ignored Casper, his lead began to melt away.

Palmer says Casper "probably wasn't the fanciest shot-maker that I ever played with, but he was a guy who had a feel for what he could do and was able to do it." That's exactly how Casper beat Palmer at the Olympic Club. While Palmer was attacking the golf course and firing at flagsticks, Casper was hitting to the centers of the greens and rolling in 30-footers for birdie.

With one hole left, they were even. Palmer's heroic par save from the rough at the 72nd hole forced an 18-hole playoff, but the extra round was a virtual replay of the preceding day. The back nine saw a six-shot turnaround in Casper's favor, and Palmer's best chance to add an eighth major title to his collection disappeared.

Ultimately, though, it was heartbreak, as much as euphoria that endeared Palmer to his fans. Nicklaus and Player commanded respect, but Palmer elicited adulation.

The scene at the 2002 Masters was almost surreal. Palmer announced after the first round that this Masters would be his last as a competitor. On Friday afternoon, Palmer drew the largest gallery at Augusta, even though Woods' name appeared at the top of the leaderboard.

Rain interrupted Palmer's farewell, and when the King returned to the course to complete the round on Saturday morning, the Army was 10,000 strong. It was a fitting tribute, and it seemed absolutely irrelevant that Palmer was shooting in the 80s.

Woods can amaze the world with his extraordinary shot-making. He can win majors by the handful. Depending on his continuing level of motivation, he may even eclipse Nicklaus' record 18 major titles. But he can only aspire to the level of adulation Palmer inspires in his faithful.

No one who saw the 2002 Masters would doubt the identity of golf's greatest generation—or its leader.

The Next Great Ones

The young guns of golf

Youth movement prepares to challenge a Tiger

In the face of Tiger Woods' all-encompassing dominance of professional golf, it wouldn't be too farfetched to find the following classified ad in the back pages of the leading national golf publications:

DESPERATELY SEEKING RIVAL — Must have game, enough to challenge the world's number one player. Must have charisma, enough to bolster TV ratings during number one player's increasingly frequent absences. Must work weekends. No base salary, but plenty of performance incentives and perks. Send resume to PGA Tour, 112 PGA Tour Blvd., Ponte Vedra Beach, FL 32082.

The Tour already has interviewed a parade of applicants. Phil Mickelson was hired on a three-year trial basis, but it now appears likely he won't work out. Vijay Singh showed promise, as did Ernie Els, but the pressure of the job seem to have taken its toll. (Both suffered nervous breakdowns in the 2002 Masters.)

David Duval was employee-of-the-year in 1999, but 10 weeks of sick leave in 2000 sapped his strength and broke his momentum. Grant Waite and Bob May showed unexpected promise, but those two short-term sensations were victims of early burnout.

Unable to promote a veteran employee from within, the Tour must look to its new faces for a potential challenger to Woods. The frontrunner for the position appears to be Spaniard Sergio Garcia, a two-time winner on Tour in 2001, at age 21. Garcia certainly has the charisma. In the 1999 PGA Championship at Medinah Country Club, Garcia chased Woods throughout the weekend and finished second.

He also chased his golf ball up the 16th fairway after extricating it from the root system of a tree in the right rough. Garcia's sprint toward the green, which included a road-runner-style jump as he strained to see his ball, was more memorable than any shot Woods hit during the tournament.

Garcia has the playing credentials, too. As a

Sergio Garcia appears to be the most imminent threat to Tiger, but he still has a few holes in his game.

Sergio Garcia (above) has the game and the personality to carry the responsibility of The Next Generation. David Gossett (opposite) has won the U.S. Amateur and had a Tour win in 2001.

17-year-old amateur, he won his first professional tournament, the Catalonian Open. Before turning pro after the 1999 Masters, he won the 1998 British Amateur Championship and made the cut in 12 of the 18 European Tour events he entered.

And despite a controversial U.S. Open in 2002, where he shot an obscene gesture at a heckler in the gallery during the second round, Garcia mounted a respectable challenge to Woods before fading on Sunday.

"It was a very positive week, I think," Garcia said after the final round. "I found my game. I played pretty well. I hung in there. It wasn't an easy week for me. It was pretty rough. But it made me mature. I think it made me stronger mentally and, you know,

it's just the way it goes sometimes, unfortunately. And I've just got to keep hanging in there and give myself as many opportunities as I can. And if I do that eventually one (major title) is going to come, and as soon as the first one comes, then everything seems a little easier."

If there's a knock on Garcia — other than his interminable re-gripping and waggling of the club as he stands over the ball — it's his swing. With an exaggerated loop at the top, Garcia lays the club off drastically as he starts his downswing. It's not the kind of move designed to promote longevity on the Tour. But others before Garcia have risen to the highest echelons of the game with swings that weren't exactly models of perfection. Arnold Palmer comes to mind.

Golfweek magazine featured Charles Howell III on one of its covers as the heir apparent to Tiger even before Howell had turned pro.

A year after Garcia won the British Amateur, Arizona's David Gossett claimed the U.S. Amateur title at Pebble Beach. A first-team All-American at the University of Texas, Gossett suffered through a difficult transition to professional golf. He missed the cut in all seven events he entered in 2000.

But Gossett earned an exemption that guarantees him two-and-a-half years on Tour with a breakthrough victory at the 2001 John Deere Classic.

"When you turn pro, things don't turn out the way you dream them up sometimes," Gossett said after the win. "But I'm 22 years of age, and I've got a win under my belt on the PGA Tour. I don't have too much to hang my head about.

"Missing seven cuts was certainly a humbling experience for me, and it's something that will make me much stronger down the road—because you dream, you go play college golf, you do well in the U.S. Amateur, and you're ready to go out there and win golf tournaments. But I had some areas that I needed to work on and become more consistent and more comfortable, and I've done that."

With his younger sister Joni as his caddy, Gossett tied for second at the 2002 Buick Classic. After a tie for 27th at the Advil Western Open in July, he was 86th on the 2002 money list with $467,433.

Perhaps no one since Garcia has arrived on Tour with as much fanfare as 2000 NCAA champion Charles Howell III, who graced the cover of Golfweek as a pretender to Tiger's throne before he ever teed it up as a member of the PGA Tour.

Though Howell looks as though he could wear ankle weights and a backpack and still not get to his listed 155 pounds, he is extremely long with his driver and his irons. Putting is the area of his game that needs the most work if Howell is to develop into a consistent, long-term rival to Woods.

Howell, who quietly made 25 consecutive cuts before the streak ended at the 2002 BellSouth Classic, doesn't seem to mind the expectations that have accompanied his arrival on Tour.

"I like being in that role," Howell said. "It won't change me a whole lot, and hopefully it won't change the way I look at things and see things. But with expectations and so forth, I try to leave them off the golf course, and to play as well as I can.

> *"There's going to be days where you think you're better than Tiger Woods, and there's going to be days you think you can't come close to him. But overall, I take (the expectations) as a compliment."*
>
> *— Charles Howell III*

"There's going to be days where you think you're better than Tiger Woods, and there's going to be days you think you can't come close to him. But overall, I take (the expectations) as a compliment."

The only real negative to Howell is his 2002 clothing deal with J. Lindeberg. No matter how well he does on the golf course, it will be tough to take him seriously until he sheds the Jesper Parnevik-meets-West Side Story golf outfits.

With four victories to his credit, Notah Begay III, Woods' college teammate at Stanford, already is the most successful Native American golfer in PGA Tour history. Begay's putting style is unique—and deadly. He can stroke it effectively from the left or right side of the ball, depending on which vantage point gives him a "hook" putt.

A former Walker Cupper who holds the single-round scoring record in NCAA Championship history (62 in 1994), Begay nevertheless has experienced

significant setbacks during his brief career. A lower back injury — the result of overzealous off-season conditioning — limited Begay to 12 starts in 2001.

A year earlier, his second arrest for drunk driving cost him seven days in jail and considerable embarrassment, especially since Begay is actively involved with youth programs in his native New Mexico.

"I was the most disappointed out of anybody," Begay said. "I let down a lot of people, especially the young kids that looked up to me. But when you're faced with adverse circum-

stances, I try to handle it as best as possible and show them that not everyone is perfect; there's nobody that goes through life not making any mistakes. And if you do make a mistake, own up to it and move on."

Begay earned considerable acclaim for the forthright way he accepted responsibility for his mistake. And midway through the 2002 season, both his back and his career seemed to be on the mend. Begay made his first cut at the Canon Greater Hartford Open in June and followed that a week later with a third-place finish in the Fed-Ex St. Jude Classic.

"I'm a 23-year-old kid, hardly just two years out of school, and now here I am, champion of the Honda Classic."

— Matt Kuchar

There were few who didn't second-guess Matt Kuchar's decision to return to Georgia Tech after the 1997 U.S. Amateur champion's sensational showings in the 1998 Masters and U.S. Open. Disdaining a pro career Kuchar, spent two more seasons at Tech—where he played second fiddle to teammate Bryce Molder.

When he finally turned pro after graduating in 2000, Kuchar, known as "Smiley" on Tour for his indefatigable good humor, couldn't find the form he had shown as an amateur. After bouncing around from Australia to Mexico to Canada to the BUY.COM Tour, Kuchar played his way onto the PGA Tour in 2001 with $572,669 in non-member earnings, second only to Howell's $1,520,632. He ensured his exempt status through 2004 with a victory in the 2002 Honda Classic in March.

Matt Kuchar played out his collegiate career at Georgia Tech and turned pro in 2000, making the PGA Tour in 2001.

would happen. I always dreamed and knew that I would win and that I would win a lot, but I wasn't sure that it would happen this soon. I'm a 23-year-old kid, hardly just two years out of school, and now here I am, champion of the Honda Classic. It's exciting for me. I'm thrilled."

Though his accurate iron game and touch around the greens are world-class, Kuchar may have trouble in the majors because he can't keep up with the really big hitters off the tee. But he should be a solid member of the Tour for years to come.

Molder likewise has been impressive in his quest for a Tour card through sponsor exemptions. In his first 11 events of 2002 he made the cut six times and earned $314,310. Molder's best finish in that stretch came at the Compaq Classic of New Orleans, where he tied for ninth.

"To win a PGA Tour event, I wasn't sure if it would happen as soon as it did," Kuchar said. "I knew it

"From about age 20 to 25—really 22 to 25—it's unbelievable how many good players in the world

Matt Kuchar (above) and Bryce Molder (opposite) were teammates at Georgia Tech, where Kuchar played second fiddle to Molder. "When I played at school with Matt Kuchar, we pushed each other."

school senior didn't become a fully vested member of the Tour until his 18th birthday, June 2, 2002.

Tryon's results thus far have been mixed. He made the cut in two of the three events he entered in 2001 —with his best finish a tie for 37th in the B.C. Open. But Tryon failed to qualify for the weekend in his first four events of 2002. Though he may prove too young to be competitive as a teenager, he'll have a wealth of experience by age 25.

Will Tryon develop the tools to challenge Woods over the next few years? For that matter, will any other member of the PGA Tour's youth movement do so?

Or will the PGA Tour once again discard the resumes of its current crop and run the same classified ad in 2005?

LPGA and Seniors Greatest

LPGA Tour

1. Kathy Whitworth
2. Mickey Wright
3. Annika Sorenstam
4. Nancy Lopez
5. Patty Berg
6. Joanne Carner
7. Louise Suggs
8. Betsy Rawls
9. Patty Sheehan
T10. Betsy King
T10. Pat Bradley
T10. Juli Inkster

Senior PGA Tour

1. Larry Nelson
2. Chi Chi Rodriguez
3. Bruce Fleisher
4. Jim Colbert
5. Gil Morgan
6. Miller Barber
7. Bob Charles
8. Don January
9. George Archer
10. Jim Thorpe

Nancy Lopez

Chi Chi Rodriguez

Index

Alphabetical roster and index of the 50 greatest golfers